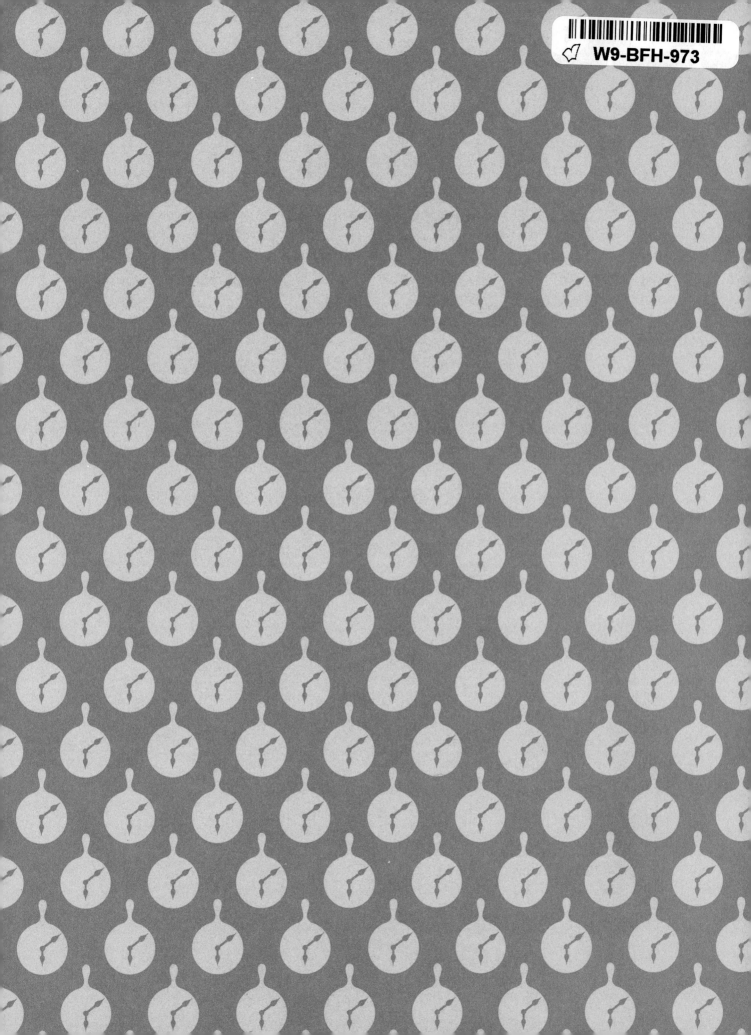

Great Meals in Minutes was created by
Rebus, Inc.
and published by Time-Life Books.

Rebus, Inc.

Publisher: Rodney Friedman
Editorial Director: Shirley Tomkievicz

Editor: Marya Dalrymple
Art Director: Ronald Gross
Senior Editor: Charles Blackwell
Food Editor and Food Stylist: Grace Young
Photographer: Steven Mays
Prop Stylist: Cathryn Schwing
Staff Writer: Alexandra Greeley
Associate Editor: Bonnie J. Slotnick
Editorial Assistant: Joan Michel
Assistant Food Stylist: Karen Hatt
Recipe Tester: Gina Palombi Barclay
Production Assistant: Lisa Young

For information about any Time-Life book,
please write:
Reader Information
Time-Life Books
541 North Fairbanks Court
Chicago, Illinois 60611
Library of Congress Cataloging in Publication Data
Meatless menus.
  (Great meals in minutes)
  Includes index.
  1. Vegetarian cookery. 2. Menus.
  3. Cooks—United States— Biography.
  I. Time-Life Books.   II. Series.
  TX837.M48 1986   641.5′636   85-16553
  ISBN 0-86706-302-5 (lib. bdg.)
  ISBN 0-86706-301-7 (retail ed.)

Second printing. Printed in U.S.A.
Published simultaneously in Canada.
School and library distribution by Silver Burdett
Company, Morristown, New Jersey.
TIME-LIFE is a trademark of Time Incorporated
U.S.A.

SERIES CONSULTANT
Margaret E. Happel is the author of *Ladies'
Home Journal Adventures in Cooking*,
*Ladies' Home Journal Handbook of Holiday
Cuisine*, and other best-selling cookbooks, as
well as the translator and adapter of Rebecca
Hsu Hiu Min's *Delights of Chinese Cooking*. A
food consultant based in New York City, she
has been director of the food department of
Good Housekeeping and editor of *American
Home* magazine.

WINE CONSULTANT
Tom Maresca combines a full-time career
teaching English literature with writing
about and consuming fine wines. He is the
author of *Mastering Wine a Taste at a Time*.

Cover: Barbara Chernetz's cheese enchiladas
with cumin rice and a tomatillo salad. See
pages 36–43.

Great Meals
IN MINUTES
MEATLESS
MENUS

TIME-LIFE BOOKS, ALEXANDRIA, VIRGINIA

Contents

Meet the Cooks

LINDA M. JOHNSON

As a behavioral nutritionist, Linda Johnson teaches overweight people new eating habits. She is the founder and director of Mind Over Matter, a nutrition and weight-management program in the San Francisco Bay Area, and a member of the American Heart Association. She was a contributing nutrition editor for *Women's Sports* and *Glamour.*

VICKI POTH

After graduating from the University of Oregon, Vicki Poth moved to New York to take a job as publicity coordinator for *Mademoiselle* magazine. She then worked as an account executive for a major public relations firm, developing and executing proposals for food accounts. In 1980 she returned to *Mademoiselle* as a food and nutrition editor, a position she continues to hold today.

BARBARA CHERNETZ

Barbara Chernetz, who holds a Master's Degree in nutrition from New York University, began her culinary career as a food stylist with Cary Kitchens in New York. She was test kitchen editor at *Cuisine* magazine before joining *Redbook* as test kitchen manager and associate food editor. At present, she is executive editor of *Good Food* magazine.

DEBORAH MADISON

Deborah Madison grew up in a farming community in central California. In 1979 she helped found Greens, a vegetarian restaurant in San Francisco, where she was also head chef. She has taught cooking classes and catered in the Bay Area, and has lived in Rome, where she studied Italian cuisine. She is currently working on the *Greens Cookbook.*

JEANNE JONES

Throughout her food career, native Californian Jeanne Jones has combined nutrition and gastronomy. She is the menu consultant to the Canyon Ranch Spa in Tucson, Arizona, and has designed the low-calorie alternative menu for the Four Seasons hotel chain. She is also the author of thirteen books, including *The Calculating Cook* and *Secrets of Salt-Free Cooking*. Her syndicated column, *Cook It Light*, appears in 300 newspapers nationwide.

JOHN ROBERT MASSIE

Midwesterner John Robert Massie, who lives in New York City, is the third generation of his family in the food business. Besides studying hotel and restaurant management, he has completed the Grand Diplôme course at L'Ecole de Cuisine La Varenne in Paris, worked with a professional caterer, and apprenticed at the Four Seasons Restaurant. He is a former director of the test kitchen at *Food & Wine* magazine and is currently designing kitchens.

URSULA FOREM AND HIDEHIKO TAKADA

Trained in Japan, Hidehiko Takada has been a master chef for thirty years. Now a resident of New York City, he runs Takada's Japanese Cooking School, where he teaches updated Japanese cooking methods. Ursula Forem, who has a long-standing interest in Japanese culture, has studied with Chef Takada for the past four years. She is currently working with him on all aspects of catering, menu planning, and teaching.

JULIE SAHNI

Born in India and now a resident of New York City, Julie Sahni spends much of her time teaching Americans about Indian food. She travels widely as a lecturer and guest chef, and writes regularly for many national food magazines. In addition, she is founder/director of her own cooking school, author of *Classic Indian Vegetarian and Grain Cooking*, and executive chef of the Nirvana restaurants in Manhattan.

ROBERT PUCCI

Robert Pucci lives in Austin, Texas, and runs Pasta by Pucci, a catering business specializing in Italian cooking. He also cooks for several families. He has lived in Italy, studying and sampling the country's regional dishes, and is now teaching Italian at the University of Texas and working on a pasta cookbook.

Meatless Menus in Minutes

GREAT MEALS FOR FOUR IN AN HOUR OR LESS

Baby eggplants. Whole-wheat flour. Buffalo mozzarella. Tofu. Black, brown, red, green, and white lentils. Raw peanuts. Pasta in novel shapes. Once considered rather exotic, these foods are currently at the heart of contemporary America's dietary revolution and have become as widely available in supermarkets as they are in health food stores and specialty food shops.

In response to mounting medical evidence linking ultra-fatty diets to heart disease and obesity, many Americans are changing their eating habits to cut back on or eliminate meat. They are preparing lighter, fresher meals low in saturated fats and calories, high in fiber-filled complex carbohydrates, and rich in vitamins, minerals, and other essential nutrients. They are replacing meat with such alternative sources of protein as nuts, seeds, low-fat dairy products, and legumes. And as a result, many men and women are pointing proudly to their leaner, trimmer bodies and boasting of their increased energy levels.

A meatless diet is hardly a modern-day phenomenon. Centuries ago, the Greek philosopher Plato observed in *The Republic* that those who follow a meatless diet "may be expected to live in peace and health to a good old age." Well before Plato, ancient cultures adhered to meatless regimens for philosophical, social, or economic reasons. Although in the last century vegetarian movements in England and America attracted a staunch following, it is only in the last few decades that great numbers of people have begun to embrace the idea of not eating meat.

Indeed, a truly positive attitude toward meatless eating exists today in this country. We have rediscovered the joys of fresh vegetables and fruits; we appreciate the versatility of yogurt and tofu and beans; we line up at salad bars to compose lunches and dinners of greens and grains. But most important, we realize that meals based on eggs, cheese, nuts, pasta, or vegetables and fruits can be *delicious* as well as healthful.

On the following pages, ten of America's most talented cooks present 27 complete menus featuring ideas for meatless meals, from a vegetable pot pie in puff pastry to egg crêpes pizza-style with assorted vegetables and goat cheese. There are international recipes for Japanese fried tofu and Italian cheese and mushroom salad as well as for Mexican vegetable hash and Greek vegetable casserole. Many of these dishes can be served either hot or cold and can be prepared well in advance of serving. A number of menus also work as lunches or brunches.

Each menu, which serves four people, can be prepared in an hour or less, and the cooks focus on a new kind of American cuisine that borrows ideas and techniques from around the world but also values our native traditions. They use fresh produce, with no powdered sauces or other dubious shortcuts. The other ingredients called for (vinegars, spices, herbs, and so on) are all of high quality and are usually available in supermarkets or specialty food stores.

The cooks and the kitchen staff have meticulously planned and tested the menus for appearance as well as for taste, as the accompanying photographs show: The vegetables are brilliant and fresh, the visual combinations appetizing. The table settings feature bright colors, simple flower arrangements, and attractive but not necessarily expensive serving dishes.

For each menu, the Editors, with advice from the cooks, suggest wines and other beverages. And there are suggestions for the use of leftovers and for complementary dishes and desserts. On each menu page, you will find a number of other tips, from an easy method for making food-processor pesto to instructions for making *crème fraîche* at home.

Because the menus in this volume contain so many different ingredients, specific information on those ingredients is provided in the introductions to the various menus. On the pages immediately following, you will find general information on buying, preparing, and storing the basic staples of meatless meals.

BEFORE YOU START

Great Meals in Minutes is designed for efficiency and ease. This book will work best for you if you follow these simple suggestions:

1. Refresh your memory with the few simple cooking techniques on the following pages. They will quickly become second nature, and you will produce professional-quality meals in minutes.

2. Read the menus before you shop. Each lists the ingredients you will need, in the order that you would expect to shop for them. Many items will already be on your pantry shelf.

Linda Johnson's pasta with stir-fried vegetables is just one example of the many low-fat, high-fiber, nutrient-filled dishes that can be made without meat (see her recipe, page 19). On the counter as well, the makings of more healthful meatless meals: vegetables and fruits, eggs and cheese, nuts, hearty bread, and a variety of legumes.

3. Check the equipment list on page 14. Good sharp knives and pots and pans of the right shape and material are essential for making great meals in minutes. This may be the time to buy a few things: The right equipment can turn cooking from a necessity into a creative experience.

4. Set out everything you need before you start to cook. The lists at the beginning of each menu tell just what is required. To save effort, always keep your ingredients in the same place so you can reach for them instinctively.

5. Follow the start-to-finish steps for each menu. That way, you can be sure of having the entire meal ready to serve in an hour.

STAPLES FOR MEATLESS MEALS

Fresh produce: Although fresh produce is available at virtually every supermarket nationwide, its quality is never guaranteed. Climate, soil, and sunshine affect fruit and vegetables, as does the care they get during harvesting, packing, and shipping. Also, the time lapse between picking and eating affects appearance, taste, and nutritive value. Produce starts to deteriorate as soon as it is picked. The best advice, therefore, is to buy produce locally during its natural growing season, either from a farmer's market or from a greengrocer supplied by local farmers. When you shop at the supermarket, remember that markets vary in their selection and handling of fresh fruits and vegetables. Find a market that offers seasonal and local items, then shop carefully, examining produce for any signs of age or decay. Buy only crisp, firm, fresh-looking produce.

Canned or frozen fruits and vegetables are rarely as good as freshly picked produce. If the fresh fruit or vegetable you want is out of season, try to find another with a similar taste and texture. The directions accompanying each menu in this book usually include suggestions for substitutions. In some cases, canned or frozen foods are acceptable alternatives: Canned tomatoes are as good as fresh ones for soups and sauces, and frozen berries are fine for certain desserts.

Many fresh vegetables can be stored for up to a week if kept wrapped in plastic in the coldest part of the refrigerator. Exceptions are onions and garlic, potatoes, sweet potatoes, turnips, and hard-shell squash, which should be kept in a cool dry spot away from direct light. Onions should not be stored near potatoes because they absorb moisture from the potatoes, which causes them to decay.

Fresh vegetables are most nutritious when eaten raw or when steamed on a wire rack or collapsible vegetable steamer in a tightly covered pot until crisp-tender. Alternatively, stir frying—the Chinese quick cooking method requiring minimal oil—is ideal for cooking bite-size, shredded, or thinly sliced portions of vegetables. (See pages 10 and 11 for more information on both cooking methods.)

Legumes: Rich in protein, B vitamins, and various minerals, legumes (also known as pulses) include hundreds of varieties of dried beans, peas, and lentils. Extremely versatile, legumes can be used in soups, stews, entrées, salads, and dips. Whether you buy beans, peas, or lentils packaged or in bulk at a supermarket or health food store, look for those that are consistent in size and color and free of mold. Stored in tightly closed containers in a cool dry place, they will last up to a year.

Most of the legumes called for in this volume have been precooked, then canned, but if you have the time you can cook the dried legumes yourself. Except for lentils and split peas, legumes require presoaking and their cooking time can be lengthy. To prepare dried legumes at home, first pick out any bits of debris, then place the legumes in a bowl and cover them with cold water. After a minute or two remove any that float to the surface. Rinse the legumes under cold running water.

For 2 to 2½ cups cooked legumes, soak 1 cup dried in 3 cups cold water for 6 hours or overnight. After soaking, drain the legumes and rinse again. Place them in a heavy pot, add 3 cups water, and bring to a boil. Simmer, partially covered, up to 3 hours, or until tender. (Be sure to check the pot and add water as necessary.) Add salt to taste at the last moment, since it can toughen legumes. In her Menu 2, page 20, Linda Johnson suggests cooking your own beans for her two-bean chili if you have the time.

Grains and pasta: Low in fat and high in fiber, grains and pasta add texture and protein to meals while serving as a foil for imaginative seasonings, sauces, and dressings.

Making Stock

A good stock is the foundation for most soups and stews in this volume, and is also an excellent base for sauces. Although canned stock or broth is acceptable to use when you are short on time, homemade stock has a rich flavor that is hard to match. Moreover, canned products are likely to be overly salty. Homemade stock is not difficult to make. The following pointers will ensure a rich, clear stock, no matter which type you make.

Use a large nonaluminum stockpot or saucepan. Stir the stock as little as possible to prevent clouding. Watch carefully to make sure the stock stays at a simmer but does not boil. Once cooked, cool the stock as quickly as possible, preferably by placing the pan in a sinkful of cold water. Do not cover it as it cools, and refrigerate it in jars or freezer containers (1-cup sizes are convenient) as soon as it has cooled. After several hours of refrigeration, any fat will congeal at the top of the stock; it may be removed or left as a protective covering. Stock will keep for up to three days in the refrigerator and up to three months in the freezer.

Chicken Stock

Save chicken parts as they accumulate and freeze them. The yellow onion skin adds color; the optional veal bone adds extra flavor and richness.

3 pounds bony chicken parts, such as wings,
  back, and neck
1 veal knuckle (optional)
Yellow onion, unpeeled and stuck with 2 whole cloves
2 stalks celery with leaves, halved
12 peppercorns
2 carrots, peeled and cut into 2-inch lengths
4 sprigs parsley
1 bay leaf
1 tablespoon chopped fresh thyme, or 1 teaspoon dried
Salt

1. Wash chicken parts, and veal knuckle if using, and drain. Place in stockpot with remaining ingredients (except salt) and add 3 quarts cold water. Cover pot and bring to a boil over medium heat.
2. Reduce heat and simmer stock, partially covered, 2 to 3 hours, skimming foam and scum from surface several times. Add salt to taste after stock has cooked 1 hour.
3. Strain stock through fine sieve placed over large bowl. Discard solids. Let stock cool uncovered; refrigerate when completely cool. *Yield:* About 10 cups

For many of the meals in this volume, you may prefer to use vegetable rather than chicken stock, particularly when you want to intensify the vegetable flavor of a recipe. A properly prepared vegetable stock, made from an assortment of fresh vegetables, is a flavorful base for a variety of soups, stews, or braised vegetable dishes. Unlike meat stocks, a vegetable stock cooks quickly because there are no bones to simmer or fat to skim off. For a richly flavored stock, vary the types of vegetables you use: Carrots, cabbage, and parsnips are sweet; leeks, celery, turnips, and onions are aromatic. Wash all vegetables, and peel them when necessary. To cook the vegetables quickly and to draw out the maximum amount of flavor, coarsely chop them either by hand or in a blender or food processor. To add extra flavor to the stock, you can include bay leaves, peppercorns, parsley, and garlic, as well as an assortment of herbs, such as a pinch of thyme, basil, or tarragon.

Vegetable Stock

2 leeks, white part only
3 carrots
2 stalks celery
2 or 3 yellow onions
3 or 4 cloves garlic
1 turnip (optional)
1 parsnip (optional)
6 sprigs parsley
1 bay leaf
1 teaspoon salt
6 whole peppercorns
½ teaspoon dried thyme, tarragon, or basil

1. Trim root ends from leeks, halve leeks lengthwise, and wash thoroughly under cold running water. Pat leeks dry and chop coarsely. Place leeks in large soup kettle or stockpot.
2. Wash carrots and celery. Peel carrots. Trim and coarsely chop carrots and celery and add to stockpot.
3. Peel and quarter onions, reserving skins. Peel garlic cloves. Add onions and garlic to stockpot. Add onion skins, if desired, to give stock a natural golden color.
4. If using turnip or parsnip, peel, trim, chop, and add to stockpot.
5. Add remaining ingredients and enough cold water to cover (approximately 1½ quarts). Cover pot and bring liquid to a boil over medium heat.
6. Lower heat and simmer, partially covered, about 1 hour.
7. Strain stock and refrigerate if not using immediately.

Such grains as rice, bulgur, buckwheat groats, and millet lend themselves to many cooking methods and are sold nationwide in supermarkets, health food stores, and specialty food shops. To slow deterioration, store grains in tightly closed containers in a dark, dry spot. Julie Sahni uses a nutty-flavored Indian rice called *basmati* in her Menu 1, page 86.

A grain product popular in hundreds of forms worldwide, pasta is most commonly sold dried in this country.

Some forms of pasta, notably Italian and Oriental noodles, are sold fresh or frozen. Fresh does not necessarily mean best where pasta is concerned, however. A high-quality, richly colored commercial dried pasta made with 100 per cent semolina flour from durum wheat is a better product than fresh pasta made from inferior ingredients. When properly cooked, quality pasta retains its satisfying texture without becoming too soft too fast. On page 99, Robert Pucci prepares manicotti with five cheeses and a topping of tomato sauce.

Tofu: For information on this high-protein meat substitute, see the box on page 11.

Nuts and seeds: Excellent sources of protein, minerals, and vitamins, nuts and seeds are particularly valued as flavor, texture, and color accents for other foods. These versatile foods also bind well with other ingredients and they can stand alone as purées or butters.

Most nuts are sold shelled or unshelled, raw or roasted. They are sold in bulk or in jars, tins, or cellophane bags. When purchasing nuts in the shell, look for those with clean, unbroken shells free of insect damage or mold. Shake a few of the nuts; if they rattle in the shell, they are probably stale. Store unshelled nuts in a cool, dry place for up to a month, or sealed in a plastic bag in the refrigerator for longer periods of time. Unshelled nuts keep longer than shelled nuts. When purchasing shelled nuts, select firm, even-colored, plump-looking nuts. When buying in bulk, taste a few, if possible. Generally, shelled nuts vacuum-packed in jars or cans are fresher than those packed in bags; if you must buy them bagged, check them once opened for any rancid odor. The nut meats should feel firm and crisp. Repackage shelled nuts in tightly closed containers and store them in the refrigerator for up to three weeks. Follow these same guidelines when selecting, purchasing, and storing seeds.

Dairy products and eggs: When shopping for any dairy product—cheese, milk, heavy or sour cream, or yogurt— or eggs, always check the product label for the expiration date. When buying eggs, open the carton to make sure that it is full and that the eggs are clean and uncracked. Damaged eggs may contain bacteria that can cause food poisoning. If any eggs crack before you get home, use them as soon as possible in a recipe that calls for them to be thoroughly cooked, such as a cake.

Cheese shops are the best sources for cheese, although a supermarket or specialty food store with a high turnover is also a good place to buy cheese. In a cheese shop, the clerks will advise you about a particular cheese and its merits and offer samples. Retailers generally receive cheese in large wheels, blocks, or cylinders. Have your cheese cut to order so you get exactly the amount you need and therefore can be confident of its quality and freshness.

To remain wholesome and tasty, all dairy products must be properly stored in the refrigerator. Eggs should be stored large end up in their carton, where they will last up to five weeks. Milk, cream, butter, and yogurt should be stored in their original containers and used as soon as possible. Hard cheese, wrapped tightly in foil or plastic and refrigerated, may keep for several weeks. Soft cheese should be kept in its container and eaten within a week.

GENERAL COOKING TECHNIQUES
Sautéing
Sautéing is a form of quick frying with no cover on the pan. In French, *sauter* means "to jump," which is what vegetables or small pieces of food do when you shake the sauté pan. The purpose is to brown the food lightly and seal in the juices, sometimes before further cooking. This technique has three critical elements: the right pan, the proper temperature, and dry food.

The sauté pan: A proper sauté pan is 10 to 12 inches in diameter and has 2- to 3-inch straight sides that allow you to turn the food and still keep the fat from spattering. It has a heavy bottom that can be moved back and forth across a burner easily.

The best material (and the most expensive) for a sauté pan is tin-lined copper because it is a superior heat conductor. Heavy-gauge aluminum works well but will discolor acidic foods like tomatoes. Therefore, you should not use aluminum if acidic food is to be cooked for more than 20 minutes after the initial browning. Another option is to select a heavy-duty sauté pan made of strong, heat conducting aluminum alloys. This type of professional cookware is smooth and stick resistant.

Use a sauté pan large enough to hold the food without crowding, or sauté in two batches. The heat of the fat and the air spaces around the pieces facilitate browning.

Many recipes call for sautéing first, then lowering the heat and cooking the food, covered, for an additional period of time. Be sure to buy a sauté pan with a tight-fitting cover. Make certain the handle is long and is comfortable to hold. Use a wooden spatula or tongs to keep the food moving in the pan as you shake it over the burner. If the food sticks, a metal spatula will loosen it best. Turn the food so that all surfaces come into contact with the hot fat.

Never immerse the hot pan in cold water because this will warp the metal. Allow the pan to cool slightly, then add water and let it sit until you are ready to wash it.

The fat: Half butter and half vegetable or peanut oil is perfect for most sautéing: It heats to high temperatures without burning, yet allows a rich butter flavor. For cooking, unsalted butter tastes best and adds no extra salt.

To sauté properly, heat the fat until it is hot but not smoking. When you see small bubbles on top of the fat, lower the heat because the fat is on the verge of smoking. When using butter and oil together, add the butter to the hot oil. After the foam from the melting butter subsides, you are ready to sauté. If the temperature of the fat is just right, the food will sizzle when you put it in the pan. Vicki Poth sautés vegetables and apples, page 29.

Pan Frying
In pan frying, the food cooks, uncovered, in a small amount of fat that has been preheated in a heavy skillet. This is a quick cooking method, suitable for firm vegetables, patties, and fritters. In her Menu 3, page 93, Julie Sahni pan fries eggplant slices.

Stir Frying
This basic Oriental technique requires very little oil, and the foods—which you stir continuously—fry over very high heat. Stir frying is ideal for cooking bite-size, shredded, or thinly sliced portions of vegetables, and other ingredients such as tofu. On page 19, Linda Johnson stir fries vegetables for a pasta topping.

Tofu

Eaten for centuries in Asia, tofu (bean curd) is rapidly gaining popularity in this country as a meat substitute. Tofu is made from soybeans that have been soaked, cooked, and puréed, then coagulated into curds. These curds—a chalky white residue—are pressed into pillows of soft, medium, or firm consistency, and bear no resemblance to their soybean parentage.

To the uninitiated, plain tofu is hardly love at first bite. Bland to mildly sweet, it is virtually tasteless, but its porous texture gives it the rare ability to absorb and acquire the flavor of foods or sauces cooked or served with it. Tofu becomes hot and spicy when stir fried with chilies; richly mellow when simmered gently with black bean sauce; delicately sweet when sprinkled with sesame oil and vinegar.

Tofu is also valued nutritionally. Not only is it an important protein staple (soybeans contain about 35% protein, more than any other unprocessed plant or animal food), but since the protein in tofu does not come from an animal source, it is cholesterol free. Tofu is also a good source of calcium, iron, potassium, B vitamins, vitamin E, and choline. Furthermore, it is low in calories—only about 167 per 8-ounce portion as purchased.

American cooks are learning to be highly creative with this Oriental food: Pressed and cubed, it can resemble chicken or cheese for stir frying or in soups or salads; blended, it thickens salad dressings and sauces; crumbled or mashed, it can be used as an addition to casseroles and pizzas. Some adventurous cooks even use it to make "cheesecake."

Once stocked exclusively in Asian markets, plain tofu is now carried by most supermarkets, specialty food shops, greengrocers, and health food stores. In supermarkets it is usually sold vacuum-packed or water-packed in sealed plastic containers; in Asian markets tofu is displayed in large water-filled tubs. Look for tofu that is an even eggshell white with a smooth surface (slimy tofu is old tofu). The water it is stored in should appear clear. If possible, smell the tofu; it should have a mild, fresh aroma.

Since tofu is quite perishable, after purchase rinse it in cold water, repack it in water in your own lidded nonaluminum container, and refrigerate it. If you change the water daily, the tofu will last for up to a week. Once it begins to smell or taste sour, dispose of it. Vacuum-packed tofu will keep for about a month unopened; once opened, store it the same way you would loose tofu.

To prepare tofu for cooking, drain it, then pat it dry with paper towels. Or, squeeze the tofu in a kitchen towel to remove excess water. For creamed or puréed tofu, use a blender or food processor and process it in small batches, adding extra liquid if necessary. Refrigerate or freeze the puréed tofu in a tightly closed container.

The following recipe for tofu salad dressing is an excellent addition to any cook's repertoire:

Tofu Salad Dressing

1 pound firm tofu
½ cup lemon juice
1 cup safflower or olive oil
1 teaspoon prepared horseradish
2 teaspoons Dijon mustard
2 cloves garlic, peeled
1 teaspoon salt
1 tablespoon finely chopped parsley

Place all ingredients in the container of a blender or food processor and process until thick and creamy. Turn into jar with tight-fitting lid and refrigerate until needed. Reblend with a whisk before serving.

Braising
Braising is simmering foods in a relatively small amount of liquid, usually for a long period of time. Sometimes the food is browned or parboiled before braising. You may wish to flavor the braising liquid with herbs, spices, and aromatic vegetables, or use wine, stock, or tomato sauce as a medium. Jeanne Jones braises tomatoes in her Menu 3, page 61.

Blanching
Blanching, or parboiling, is an invaluable technique. Immerse vegetables for a few moments in boiling water, then refresh them, that is, plunge them into cold water to stop their cooking and set their colors. Blanching softens or tenderizes dense or hard vegetables, often as a preliminary to further cooking by another method, such as stir frying. Hidehiko Takada and Ursula Forem blanch vegetables, page 83.

Steaming
Steaming is a healthful way to cook vegetables and other foods, including desserts. Bring about an inch of water to a boil in a saucepan. Place the food in a steamer or on a rack over the water and cover the pan. Keeping the food above the liquid preserves vitamins and minerals often lost in other methods of cooking. Jeanne Jones steams carrots, cauliflower, and zucchini, page 60.

Broiling
This is a relatively fast cooking method in which the food is placed directly under a heat source, producing a crisp surface while leaving the inside juicy. To add flavor or moisture, brush the food with oil or butter, a sauce, or a marinade before you cook. Barbara Chernetz broils her vegetable hash for a few minutes, page 41.

Baking
Baking applies to the dry-heat cooking of foods such as casseroles, whole or halved vegetables, and, of course, breads and pastries. Some foods are baked tightly covered to retain their juices and flavors; others, such as breads, cakes, and cookies, are baked in open pans to release moisture. Vicki Poth's Menu 3, page 33, features baked *bryami*, a Greek vegetable casserole.

Pantry (for this volume)

A well-stocked, properly organized pantry is essential for preparing great meals in the shortest time possible. Whether your pantry consists of a small refrigerator and two or three shelves over the sink, or a large freezer, refrigerator, and entire room just off the kitchen, you must protect staples from heat and light.

In maintaining your pantry, follow these rules:

1. Store staples by kind and date. Canned goods, canisters, and spices need a separate shelf, or a separate spot on a shelf. Date all staples—shelved, refrigerated, or frozen—by writing the date directly on the package or on a bit of masking tape. Then put the oldest ones in front to be sure you use them first.

2. Store flour, sugar, and other dry ingredients in canisters or jars with tight lids. Glass and clear plastic allow you to see at a glance how much remains.

3. Keep a running grocery list so that you can note when a staple is half gone, and be sure to stock up.

ON THE SHELF:

Beans, canned
cannellini
chickpeas (garbanzo beans)
kidney beans
pinto beans

Capers
Capers are usually packed in vinegar and less frequently in salt. If you use the latter, you should rinse them under cold water before using them.

Chilies, canned

Cornstarch
Less likely to lump than flour, cornstarch is an excellent thickener for sauces. Substitute in the following proportions: 1 tablespoon cornstarch to 2 of flour.

Dried fruits
figs
raisins

Flour
all-purpose, bleached or unbleached
whole wheat

Garlic
Store in a cool, dry, well-ventilated place. Garlic powder and garlic salt are not adequate substitutes for fresh garlic.

Herbs and spices
The flavor of fresh herbs is much better than that of dried. Fresh herbs should be refrigerated and used as soon as possible. The following herbs are perfectly acceptable dried, but buy in small amounts, store airtight in dry area away from heat and light, and use as quickly as possible. In measuring herbs, remember that one part dried will equal three parts fresh. Crushing dried herbs brings out their flavor: Use a mortar and pestle or sandwich the herbs between 2 sheets of waxed paper and crush with a rolling pin. *Note:* Dried chives and parsley should not be on your shelf, since they have little or no flavor; frozen chives are acceptable. Buy whole spices rather than ground, as they keep their flavor much longer. Grind spices at home and store as directed for herbs.

allspice, ground
basil
bay leaves
caraway seeds
Cayenne pepper
chili powder
chilies, whole dried
cinnamon, sticks and ground
coriander, whole and ground
cumin, whole and ground
curry powder
dill
mustard, seeds and powdered
nutmeg, whole and ground
oregano
paprika
pepper
> *black peppercorns*
> These are unripe peppercorns dried in their husks. Grind with a pepper mill for each use.
> *white peppercorns*
> These are the same as the black variety, but are picked ripe and husked. Use them in pale sauces when black pepper specks would spoil the appearance.

red pepper flakes (also called crushed red pepper)
saffron
> Made from the dried stigmas of a species of crocus, this spice—the most costly of all seasonings—adds both color and flavor. Use sparingly.

salt
> Use coarse salt—commonly available as kosher or sea—for its superior flavor, texture, and purity. Kosher salt and sea salt are less salty than table salt. Substitute in the following proportions: three-quarters teaspoon table salt equals just under one teaspoon kosher or sea salt.

tarragon
thyme
turmeric

Honey

Hot pepper sauce

Nuts and seeds
almonds
cashews
peanuts
pecans
pine nuts (pignoli)
sesame seeds
sunflower seeds
walnuts

Oils
corn, safflower, peanut, or vegetable
> Because these neutral-tasting oils have high smoking points, they are good for high-heat sautéing.

olive oil
> Sample French, Greek, Spanish, and Italian oils. Olive oil ranges in color from pale yellow to dark green and in taste from mild and delicate to rich and fruity. Different olive oils can be used for different purposes: for example, use stronger ones for cooking, lighter ones for salads. The finest quality olive oil is labeled extra-virgin or virgin.

Oriental sesame oil
> Flavorful dark amber-colored oil; for seasoning.

Olives
California pitted black olives
Kalamata olives
Oil-cured black olives

Onions
> Store all dry-skinned onions in a cool, dry, well-ventilated place.

red or Italian onions
> Zesty tasting and generally eaten raw. The perfect salad onion.

shallots
> The most subtle member of the onion family, the shallot has a delicate garlic flavor.

yellow onions
> All-purpose cooking onions, strong in taste.

Peanut butter

Potatoes, boiling and baking

Rice

long-grain white rice

Slender grains that become light and fluffy when cooked and are best for general use.

Soy sauce, Japanese

Stock, vegetable and chicken

For maximum flavor and quality, your own stock is best (see recipe page 9), but canned stock, broth, or bouillon cubes are adequate for most recipes and convenient to have on hand.

Sugar

granulated sugar

brown sugar

Tomatoes

Italian plum tomatoes

Canned plum tomatoes (preferably imported) are an acceptable substitute for fresh.

Sun-dried, oil-packed tomatoes (*pumate*)

tomato paste

Spoon single tablespoons of unused canned paste onto wax paper and freeze them. Lift frozen paste off and store in plastic container. Sometimes available in tubes, which can be stored in the refrigerator after a small amount is used.

Vinegars

red and white wine vinegars

rice vinegar

tarragon vinegar

Wines and spirits

red wine, dry

Worcestershire sauce

IN THE REFRIGERATOR:

Basil

Though fresh basil is widely available only in summer, try to use it whenever possible to replace dried; the flavor is markedly superior. Stand the stems, preferably with roots intact, in a jar of water, and loosely cover leaves with a plastic bag.

Bread crumbs

You need never buy bread crumbs. To make fresh crumbs, use fresh or day-old bread and process in food processor or blender. For dried, toast bread 30 minutes in preheated 250-degree oven, turning occasionally to prevent slices from browning. Proceed as for fresh. Store bread crumbs in an airtight container: fresh crumbs in the refrigerator and dried crumbs in a cool, dry place. Either type may also be frozen for several weeks in a tightly sealed plastic bag.

Butter

Many cooks prefer unsalted butter because of its finer flavor and because it does not burn as easily as salted.

Cheese

Cheddar, sharp

A firm cheese, ranging in color from nearly white to yellow. Cheddar is a versatile cooking cheese.

Goat cheese

French-style goat cheese, or *chèvre*, has a distinct tanginess, though it is quite mild when young. Domestic *chèvres* are less salty than the imported ones. Feta is a sharp, crumbly Greek goat cheese aged and packed in brine.

Monterey Jack

From California—a mild cheese made from skim, partly skim, or whole milk.

Mozzarella

A mild cheese, most commonly made from cow's milk. Fresh mozzarella is far superior to packaged and can generally be found in Italian grocery stores.

Parmesan cheese

Avoid the pre-grated packaged variety; it is very expensive and almost flavorless. Buy Parmesan by the piece and grate as needed: 4 ounces produces about one cup of grated cheese.

Provolone

Similar to mozzarella in texture, provolone has a mellow, smoky flavor.

Ricotta

A soft fresh cheese resembling cottage cheese. Available as a whole- or skimmed-milk product.

Romano

This sharp Italian grating cheese may be made from sheep's milk (pecorino Romano) or cow's milk.

Chilies, fresh

Coriander

Also called *cilantro* or Chinese parsley, its pungent leaves resemble flat-leaf parsley. Refrigerate in a glass of water covered with a plastic bag.

Cream

heavy cream

sour cream

Eggs

Will keep 4 to 5 weeks in refrigerator. For best results, bring to room temperature before using, except when separating.

Ginger, fresh

Found in the produce section. Wrap in a paper towel, then in plastic, and refrigerate; it will keep for about 1 month, but should be checked weekly for mold. Or, if you prefer, store it in the freezer, where it will last about 3 months. Firm, smooth-skinned ginger need not be peeled.

Ketchup

Lemons

In addition to its many uses in cooking, a slice of lemon rubbed over cut apples and pears will keep them from discoloring. Do not substitute bottled juice or lemon extract.

Limes

Milk

Mint

Fresh mint will keep for a week if wrapped in a damp paper towel and enclosed in a plastic bag.

Mustard

The recipes in this book usually call for Dijon or coarse-grained mustard.

Parsley

The two most commonly available kinds of parsley are flat-leaf and curly; they can be used interchangeably when necessary. Flat-leaf parsley has a more distinctive flavor and is generally preferred in cooking. Curly parsley wilts less easily and is excellent for garnishing. Store parsley in a glass of water and cover loosely with a plastic bag. It will keep for a week in the refrigerator. Or wash and dry it, and refrigerate in a small plastic bag with a dry paper towel inside to absorb any moisture.

Scallions

Tofu

Most recipes in this volume call for firm Chinese-style tofu.

Yogurt

Equipment

Proper cooking equipment makes the work light and is a good cook's most prized possession. You can cook expertly without a store-bought steamer or even a food processor, but basic pans, knives, and a few other items are indispensable. Below are the things you need—and some attractive options—for preparing the menus in this volume.

Pots and pans
Stockpot with cover
3 skillets (large, medium, small) with covers; one with oven-proof handle
8-inch nonstick skillet
3 saucepans with covers (1-, 2-, and 4-quart capacities)
Choose heavy-gauge enameled cast-iron, plain cast-iron, aluminum-clad stainless steel, or aluminum (but you need at least one saucepan that is not aluminum). Best—but very expensive—is tin-lined copper.
2-quart baking dish
2-quart soufflé dish
13 x 9-inch baking dish
17 x 11-inch baking sheet
Metal pie pan
Jelly-roll pan
Flameproof casserole with cover
Salad bowl

Knives
A carbon-steel knife takes a sharp edge but tends to rust. You must wash and dry it after each use; otherwise it can blacken foods and counter tops. Good-quality stainless-steel knives, frequently honed, are less trouble and will serve just as well in the home kitchen. Never put a fine knife in the dishwasher. Rinse it, dry it, and put it away—but not loose in a drawer. Knives will stay sharp if they have their own storage rack.
Small paring knife
10-inch chef's knife
Bread knife (serrated edge)
Sharpening steel

Other cooking tools
2 sets of mixing bowls in graduated sizes, one set preferably glass or stainless steel
2 sets of measuring cups and spoons in graduated sizes
One for dry ingredients, another for shortenings and liquids.

Colander with a round base (stainless steel, aluminum, or enamel)
2 strainers, coarse and fine mesh
Slotted spoon
Long-handled wooden spoons
Ladle
2 metal spatulas or turners (for lifting hot foods from pans)
Rubber or vinyl spatula (for folding in ingredients)
Grater (metal, with several sizes of holes)
A rotary grater is handy for hard cheese.
Wire whisk
Pair of metal tongs
Wooden board
Garlic press
Vegetable peeler
Vegetable brush
Collapsible vegetable steamer
Mortar and pestle
Pastry brush for basting (a small, new paintbrush that is not nylon serves well)
Melon baller
Kitchen shears
Kitchen timer
Cheesecloth
Aluminum foil
Paper towels
Plastic wrap
Waxed paper
Kitchen string
Oven mitts or potholders
Thin rubber gloves

Electric appliances
Food processor or blender
A blender will do most of the work required in this volume, but a food processor will do it more quickly and in larger volume. A food processor should be considered a necessity, not a luxury, for anyone who enjoys cooking.
Electric mixer

Optional cooking tools
Salad spinner
Small jar with tight-fitting lid
Spice grinder
Salad servers
Citrus juicer
Inexpensive glass kind from the dime store will do.
Nutmeg grater
Roll of masking tape or white paper tape for labeling and dating

SHARPENING STEEL

CHEF'S KNIFE

PARING KNIFE

COLANDER

STRAINER

FOOD PROCESSOR

RUBBER SPATULA

WHISK

METAL SPATULA

MIXING BOWLS

VEGETABLE PEELER

TONGS

CASSEROLE

STOCKPOT

SAUCEPANS

SOUFFLÉ DISH

SKILLET

Linda M. Johnson

Nutritionist Linda Johnson says vegetables are "a healthful addition to any meal because they are low in fat, sugar, and salt, and full of many important nutrients as well as fiber." When planning meals, she assesses recipes for their fat, sodium, and fiber content, then mixes and matches dishes to achieve a good balance.

Menu 1 incorporates pasta, which is low in fat, with fresh asparagus, tomatoes, and protein-rich pecans. The pasta is preceded by an eggplant appetizer served on thin slices of French bread and is accompanied by a vegetable and *enoki* mushroom salad with a light honey-grapefruit dressing.

In Menu 2, the beans in the chili, the whole-wheat pastry flour in the popovers, and the spinach and radish salad with whole-grain croutons provide a healthy and palate-pleasing variety of tastes and textures. Because the tomato purée used in the chili is relatively high in sodium, Linda Johnson adds no salt to that recipe.

Menu 3 features dishes that sound and taste rich even though they are not. The red bell pepper soup, for example, is thickened with ricotta instead of the traditional heavy cream, and the shredded-vegetable pancakes are topped with a yogurt sauce rather than one made with sour cream.

Warm, subtly seasoned eggplant spread on French bread is an appealing prelude to the hearty main course of pasta with stir-fried vegetables and a salad of butter lettuce, chickpeas, enoki *mushrooms, red pepper, and carrot.*

16

Eggplant Canapés
Pasta with Stir-Fried Vegetables
Vegetable and Mushroom Salad with Honey-Grapefruit Dressing

The pasta with stir-fried vegetables is accented by the addition of Italian sun-dried tomatoes, or *pumate*, and their oil. Sun-dried tomatoes are sold loose or in jars at specialty food shops and Italian groceries. Although they are costly, these highly flavorful tomatoes are well worth including. There is no substitute for them in this recipe. The pasta dish also calls for 1 to 4 ounces of feta cheese. Because this cheese can be quite salty, the cook prefers to use the lesser amount, but provides a range for those who like more cheese.

The vegetable salad, dressed with a tangy citrus mixture, contains Japanese *enoki* (or *enokitake*) mushrooms, which resemble tiny ivory-colored umbrellas. Look for *enoki* in well-stocked supermarkets and Oriental groceries. Refrigerate them in the original package, or wrapped in paper towels, and use them as soon as possible. If they are unavailable, substitute thinly sliced white mushrooms.

If you wish, and have the time, lightly toast the French bread slices for the eggplant appetizer.

WHAT TO DRINK

The cook suggests a white Zinfandel here. For a drier wine, try a California Sauvignon Blanc or an Alsatian Sylvaner.

SHOPPING LIST AND STAPLES

1 pound asparagus
Small eggplant (about ¾ pound)
Small head butter lettuce
¼-pound package enoki mushrooms, if available
½ pound white mushrooms, plus ¼ pound if not using enoki
Small red bell pepper
Medium-size carrot
Medium-size yellow onion
Small red onion (about ¼ pound)
1 large and 4 medium-size cloves garlic
Small grapefruit
Large lemon
2 large eggs
1 to 4 ounces feta cheese
8-ounce can chickpeas
2-ounce jar capers
6-ounce can tomato paste

6½-ounce jar oil-cured black olives
6½-ounce jar oil-packed sun-dried tomatoes
⅓ cup safflower oil
3 tablespoons good-quality olive oil
2 tablespoons red wine vinegar
1 teaspoon Worcestershire sauce
1 tablespoon honey
¾ pound egg-enriched linguine or tagliarini
Long loaf French bread (baguette)
¼ cup pecan pieces
1 teaspoon sugar
1 teaspoon dried oregano
½ teaspoon dry mustard
¼ teaspoon dried basil
Salt and freshly ground black and white pepper

UTENSILS

Large stockpot
Large heavy-gauge skillet or wok
10-inch heavy-gauge skillet
3 small bowls, 1 nonaluminum
Colander
Strainer
Measuring cups and spoons
Chef's knife
Bread knife (optional)
Paring knife
2 wooden spoons
Citrus juicer (optional)
Whisk
Vegetable peeler

START-TO-FINISH STEPS

1. Wipe white mushrooms clean with damp paper towels. Coarsely chop enough to measure 2 cups for eggplant recipe. Thinly slice enough to measure 1 cup if using for salad recipe. Trim enoki mushrooms, if using. Peel onions. Coarsely chop enough yellow onion to measure about ¾ cup for eggplant recipe. Cut red onion into ¼-inch-thick rings for pasta recipe. Peel and mince 2 medium-size cloves garlic for eggplant recipe. Crush and peel 2 medium-size cloves for pasta recipe, and large clove for dressing recipe. Halve lemon and squeeze enough juice to measure 3 tablespoons for pasta recipe. Halve grapefruit and squeeze enough juice to measure ⅓ cup for dressing.

2. Follow eggplant recipe steps 1 and 2.

3. While vegetables are cooking, follow pasta recipe steps 1 and 2.

4. Follow eggplant recipe step 3.

5. While vegetables continue to cook, follow salad recipe steps 1 and 2 and dressing recipe step 1.

6. Follow eggplant recipe step 4 and pasta recipe step 3.

7. While water is coming to a boil, follow eggplant recipe step 5 and serve as first course.

8. Follow salad recipe step 3 and pasta recipe steps 4 through 8.

9. Follow dressing recipe step 2, salad recipe step 4, and serve with pasta.

RECIPES

Eggplant Canapés

Small eggplant (about ¾ pound)
2 tablespoons capers
3 tablespoons good-quality olive oil
¾ cup coarsely chopped yellow onion
½ pound white mushrooms, coarsely chopped
2 medium-size cloves garlic, peeled and minced
6-ounce can tomato paste
2 tablespoons red wine vinegar
1 teaspoon Worcestershire sauce
1 teaspoon sugar
1 teaspoon dried oregano
½ teaspoon freshly ground black pepper
Long loaf French bread (baguette)

1. Wash eggplant and dry with paper towels. Trim eggplant and cut into ½-inch dice. You should have about 4 cups. Drain capers in strainer.

2. Heat olive oil in 10-inch heavy-gauge skillet over medium heat until hot. Add eggplant, onion, mushrooms, and garlic, and cook, stirring often, 10 minutes.

3. Add capers, tomato paste, vinegar, ¼ cup water, Worcestershire sauce, sugar, oregano, and pepper, and stir well to combine. Simmer, stirring occasionally, 10 minutes.

4. Remove skillet from heat. Cut bread into ½-inch-thick slices and spread with eggplant mixture.

5. Arrange canapés on platter and serve.

Pasta with Stir-Fried Vegetables

1 pound asparagus
6½-ounce jar oil-cured black olives
1½ ounces oil-packed sun-dried tomatoes (about 6 whole), including 2 tablespoons oil
1 to 4 ounces feta cheese
2 large eggs
¼ teaspoon dried basil
3 tablespoons lemon juice
¾ pound egg-enriched linguine or tagliarini
2 medium-size cloves garlic, crushed and peeled

Small red onion, cut into ¼-inch-thick rings
¼ cup pecan pieces

1. Wash asparagus and dry with paper towels. Trim and discard woody ends and cut stalks crosswise into 1-inch pieces. Drain ¾ cup olives. Pit olives and slice lengthwise. 2 tablespoons oil, and coarsely chop enough tomatoes to measure ¼ cup. Crumble feta to taste into large serving bowl. Beat eggs lightly in small bowl.

2. Add olives, tomatoes, basil, and lemon juice to feta in large bowl; set aside.

3. Bring 3 quarts water to a boil in large stockpot over high heat.

4. Add pasta to boiling water and cook according to package directions until *al dente*.

5. Meanwhile, heat reserved oil from tomatoes in large heavy-gauge skillet or wok over medium-high heat until hot. Add garlic and stir fry until browned. Discard garlic.

6. Add asparagus and stir fry 4 minutes. Add onion and stir fry 2 minutes. Add pecans and stir fry 1 minute. Remove pan from heat.

7. Drain pasta in colander and rinse under very hot water 15 seconds.

8. Add pasta, beaten eggs, and stir-fried vegetables to tomato mixture in serving bowl and toss well to combine.

Vegetable and Mushroom Salad with Honey-Grapefruit Dressing

Small head butter lettuce
Small red bell pepper
Medium-size carrot
¼ cup chickpeas
¼-pound package enoki mushrooms, trimmed, or 1 cup thinly sliced white mushrooms
Honey-Grapefruit Dressing (see following recipe)

1. Wash lettuce, bell pepper, and carrot and dry with paper towels. Separate lettuce leaves. Core and seed bell pepper and cut into thin rings. Peel and trim carrot. Using vegetable peeler, cut carrot into long ½-inch-wide strips.

2. Rinse and drain chickpeas in strainer.

3. Line serving platter with lettuce leaves. Top with bell pepper rings, carrot strips, chickpeas, and mushrooms.

4. Just before serving, drizzle salad with dressing.

Honey-Grapefruit Dressing

⅓ cup safflower oil
⅓ cup grapefruit juice
1 tablespoon honey
Large clove garlic, crushed and peeled
½ teaspoon dry mustard
Salt and freshly ground white pepper

1. Combine all ingredients in small nonaluminum bowl and whisk until mustard is dissolved. Let stand at room temperature until needed.

2. Before serving, discard garlic and whisk dressing briefly.

Spicy Two-Bean Chili
Parmesan Popovers
Spinach and Radish Salad

This piquant two-bean chili calls for lima beans (also known as butter beans) and *cannellini*. A variety of white kidney bean, *cannellini* are an Italian product sold dried, or precooked in cans. The recipe suggests the canned type, but you can use dried beans if time permits. Follow the cooking instructions for legumes on page 8. You can also substitute another variety of canned bean, such as pinto, Great Northern, Navy, or kidney beans for the *cannellini*. If you want a hotter chili, do not seed the jalapeño.

For a festive cold-weather buffet, offer a tureen brimming with spicy vegetable chili, and a large bowl of spinach and radish salad. A painted basket is a rustic server for the Parmesan popovers.

WHAT TO DRINK

A fruity red wine, such as a California Gamay Beaujolais or Zinfandel, is a fine match for this menu. Or, choose a French Beaujolais or Beaujolais-Villages, or an Italian Barbera or Dolcetto.

SHOPPING LIST AND STAPLES

1 pound spinach
Large bunch radishes
Large green bell pepper
Small jalapeño pepper
1 pound yellow onions
6 medium-size cloves garlic

Medium-size lemon
2 large eggs
1 cup low-fat milk
2 tablespoons unsalted butter
1 ounce Parmesan cheese, preferably imported
16-ounce can cannellini beans
16-ounce can lima beans
16-ounce can tomato purée
16-ounce can whole peeled tomatoes
3 tablespoons good-quality olive oil
2 tablespoons safflower oil
¼ teaspoon Dijon mustard
⅔ cup whole-wheat pastry flour or regular whole-wheat flour, if available
⅓ cup unbleached flour, or 1 cup if not using whole-wheat flour
2 slices whole-grain bread
Pinch of sugar
1 tablespoon hot chili powder
1½ teaspoons dried oregano
1½ teaspoons ground cumin
¼ teaspoon dried basil
Bay leaf
Salt
Freshly ground black and white pepper
½ cup dry red wine

UTENSILS

Food processor or blender
Medium-size skillet
5-quart heavy-gauge saucepan
Small saucepan or butter warmer
8-cup popover pan or 12-cup muffin pan
2 large bowls
Small nonaluminum bowl
Colander
Salad spinner (optional)
Measuring cups and spoons
Chef's knife
Paring knife
2 wooden spoons
Grater (if not using food processor)
Flour sifter
Citrus juicer (optional)
Thin rubber gloves
Toaster (optional)

START-TO-FINISH STEPS

1. Peel garlic and mince 4 cloves for chili recipe and 2 cloves for salad recipe.
2. Follow chili recipe step 1 and salad recipe step 1.

3. Follow popovers recipe steps 1 through 7.

4. While popovers bake, follow chili recipe step 2.

5. While chili simmers, follow salad recipe steps 2 through 5.

6. Follow popovers recipe step 8.

7. While popovers continue to bake, follow chili recipe step 3.

8. While chili continues to cook, follow salad recipe step 6.

9. Follow chili recipe step 4, popovers recipe step 9, and serve with salad.

RECIPES

Spicy Two-Bean Chili

Large green bell pepper
Small jalapeño pepper
1 pound yellow onions
16-ounce can cannellini beans
16-ounce can lima beans
16-ounce can whole peeled tomatoes
2 tablespoons safflower oil
4 medium-size cloves garlic, peeled
   and minced
1 tablespoon hot chili powder
2 cups canned tomato purée
½ cup dry red wine
1½ teaspoons dried oregano
1½ teaspoons ground cumin
Bay leaf
Pinch of sugar

1. Wash peppers and pat dry with paper towels. Halve, core and coarsely chop bell pepper. Wearing rubber gloves, halve, seed, and mince jalapeño. Halve and peel onions and coarsely chop enough to measure about 2½ cups. Turn cannellini and lima beans into colander, rinse under cold running water, and set aside to drain. Turn canned tomatoes and their juice into large bowl and crush with wooden spoon.

2. Heat safflower oil in 5-quart heavy-gauge saucepan over medium-high heat until hot. Add bell pepper, jalapeño, onions, garlic, and chili powder, and sauté, stirring, 4 minutes, or until vegetables are tender. Add tomatoes and their juice, tomato purée, wine, oregano, cumin, bay leaf, and sugar, and simmer, uncovered, 20 minutes.

3. Add beans and simmer, stirring gently several times, 10 minutes.

4. Discard bay leaf and transfer chili to tureen or serving bowl.

Parmesan Popovers

⅔ cup whole-wheat pastry flour or regular whole-wheat
   flour, if available
⅓ cup unbleached flour, or 1 cup if not using whole-wheat
   flour
1 tablespoon unsalted butter
1 ounce Parmesan cheese, preferably imported
1 cup low-fat milk
2 large eggs
⅛ teaspoon salt

1. Preheat oven to 450 degrees.

2. Sift flours together into large bowl. Melt butter in small saucepan over low heat.

3. Meanwhile, using food processor or grater, grate enough Parmesan to measure ¼ cup.

4. Thoroughly grease 8 popover pan cups or 10 muffin pan cups and place in oven to heat.

5. Combine melted butter, milk, eggs, and salt in container of blender or food processor and process 1 minute. With machine running, gradually add flour and process until well combined. Continue to process on high speed another minute.

6. Remove pan from oven. Pour about 2 tablespoons batter into each greased cup and top with generous teaspoon grated Parmesan. Add remaining batter, filling each cup two-thirds full. Fill any empty cups with water to prevent scorching.

7. Bake popovers 15 minutes.

8. Without opening oven, reduce temperature to 350 degrees and bake another 20 minutes, or until popovers are puffed, golden, and crisp.

9. Transfer popovers to napkin-lined basket and serve immediately.

Spinach and Radish Salad

1 pound spinach
Large bunch radishes
Medium-size lemon
2 slices whole-grain bread
3 tablespoons good-quality olive oil
¼ teaspoon Dijon mustard
¼ teaspoon dried basil
Freshly ground pepper
1 tablespoon unsalted butter
2 medium-size cloves garlic, peeled
   and minced

1. Wash spinach and dry in salad spinner or with paper towels. Trim and discard tough stems from spinach and tear leaves into bite-size pieces. You should have 4 to 5 cups. Wash and dry radishes. Trim radishes and slice thinly. Halve lemon and squeeze enough juice to measure 1½ tablespoons.

2. Toast bread in toaster or oven and cut into ½-inch cubes.

3. For dressing, place lemon juice, olive oil, mustard, basil, and pepper in small nonaluminum bowl and stir to combine. Set aside.

4. Melt butter in medium-size skillet over medium heat. Add garlic and sauté 1 minute.

5. Add bread cubes and cook 2 to 3 minutes, or until well browned. Remove pan from heat.

6. Combine spinach, radishes, and croutons in salad bowl. Stir dressing to recombine, drizzle over salad, and toss well.

Creamy Red Pepper Soup
Vegetable Pancakes with Yogurt Sauce
Steamed Broccoli with Slivered Almonds

Red pepper soup with zesty vegetable pancakes and steamed broccoli is a delightful, quick meal to end a busy day.

The flavorful red bell pepper soup can be served with the pancakes, or as a first course. The soup is thickened with part-skim ricotta, which resembles cottage cheese. It is sold in cartons in the dairy section of most supermarkets. Chopped leek is another ingredient in the soup. Although the leek is a member of the onion family, it has a delicate flavor very different from that of an ordinary yellow onion. Choose a leek with dark green leaves and a medium-size stalk; large leeks are often woody and flavorless. Be sure to wash the leek thoroughly, since sand often gets trapped deep in its layers.

The vegetable pancakes topped with spicy yogurt sauce are an unusual variation on potato pancakes. Squeezing the shredded vegetables dry helps prevent excess moisture from thinning the batter. The vegetables are bound together by two lightly beaten eggs. If the mixture does not hold together well, add an extra egg white to the batter.

WHAT TO DRINK

Try an aromatic and spicy Gewürztraminer or a fuller-bodied white such as a California Chardonnay with this meatless meal.

SHOPPING LIST AND STAPLES

2 large red bell peppers (about 1 pound total weight)
¾ pound broccoli
¾ pound all-purpose potatoes
½ pound zucchini
2 medium-size yellow onions (about 1 pound total weight)
Small leek
Small clove garlic
Small bunch fresh dill, or ¼ teaspoon dried
Small bunch fresh basil, or ½ teaspoon dried
Large lemon
2 large eggs
1 pint low-fat plain yogurt
2 tablespoons unsalted butter
2 ounces Parmesan cheese, preferably imported
8-ounce container part-skim ricotta cheese
4 cups vegetable or chicken stock, preferably homemade (see page 9), or canned
3 tablespoons vegetable oil, approximately
3 tablespoons Oriental sesame oil
½ cup slivered almonds
1 teaspoon Dijon mustard
Dash of hot pepper sauce
Pinch of sugar
¼ cup unseasoned dry bread crumbs
¼ teaspoon paprika, approximately
Salt and freshly ground black and white pepper
1 tablespoon port wine

UTENSILS

Food processor or blender
Large heavy-gauge skillet
5-quart heavy-gauge saucepan
Large saucepan with cover
Small baking sheet
Collapsible vegetable steamer
3 large bowls
3 small bowls
Colander
Measuring cups and spoons
Chef's knife
Paring knife
2 wooden spoons
Metal spatula
Rubber spatula
Ladle
Grater (if not using food processor)
Citrus juicer (optional)
Vegetable peeler

START-TO-FINISH STEPS

1. Peel onions. Coarsely chop enough onion to measure 1 cup for soup recipe and dice enough remaining onion to measure ½ cup for pancakes recipe.
2. Follow yogurt sauce recipe steps 1 and 2.
3. Follow soup recipe steps 1 through 3.
4. While soup is simmering, follow pancakes recipe steps 1 through 4.
5. Follow soup recipe step 4 and broccoli recipe steps 1 and 2.
6. Follow soup recipe step 5 and broccoli recipe step 3.
7. Follow pancakes recipe step 5, broccoli recipe step 4, and soup recipe step 6.
8. Follow broccoli recipe step 5, soup recipe step 7, pancakes recipe step 6, and serve.

RECIPES

Creamy Red Pepper Soup

2 large red bell peppers (about 1 pound total weight)
Small leek
Small bunch fresh dill, or ¼ teaspoon dried
2 tablespoons unsalted butter
1 cup coarsely chopped onion
4 cups vegetable or chicken stock
½ cup part-skim ricotta cheese
1 tablespoon port wine
Salt and freshly ground white pepper

1. Wash bell peppers and dry with paper towels. Halve, core, seed, and coarsely chop peppers. Trim and discard dark green leaves from leek. Trim root end, split leek lengthwise, and wash carefully under cold running water to remove any trapped sand or grit. Dry leek and coarsely chop enough to measure about 1 cup. Wash fresh dill, if using, and pat dry with paper towels. Set aside 4 sprigs for garnish, and mince enough remaining dill to measure 1 tablespoon.

2. Melt butter in 5-quart heavy-gauge saucepan over medium-low heat. Add bell peppers, leek, minced or dried dill, and onion, and cook, stirring frequently, 7 minutes, or until vegetables are softened.

3. Add stock and simmer, uncovered, 20 minutes.

4. Remove pan from heat and allow soup to cool 10 to 15 minutes.

5. Transfer soup in batches to food processor or blender and process until puréed. As processed, transfer soup to large bowl. Add ricotta and port to last batch and process until smooth. Add salt and pepper to taste. Return soup to saucepan.

6. Reheat soup over medium-low heat until hot. Do not allow soup to boil.

7. Ladle soup into 4 soup bowls and garnish with dill sprigs.

Vegetable Pancakes

Small bunch fresh basil, or ½ teaspoon dried
2 ounces Parmesan cheese, preferably imported
½ pound zucchini
¾ pound all-purpose potatoes
½ cup diced onion
¼ cup unseasoned dry bread crumbs
Freshly ground pepper
2 large eggs
3 tablespoons vegetable oil, approximately
Yogurt Sauce (see following recipe)
⅛ teaspoon paprika

1. Wash fresh basil, if using, and pat dry with paper towels. Mince enough leaves to measure 1 tablespoon. Using food processor or grater, grate enough Parmesan to measure ¼ cup; set aside.

2. Wash and dry zucchini and potatoes. Trim zucchini. Peel potatoes. Using food processor or grater, coarsely shred enough zucchini and potatoes to measure about 1½ cups each. Place grated vegetables in colander and squeeze with hands to remove excess moisture. Pat vegetables as dry as possible with paper towels.

3. Combine minced or dried basil, Parmesan, zucchini, potatoes, onion, bread crumbs, and pepper to taste in large bowl.

4. Break eggs into small bowl and beat lightly with fork. Add eggs to vegetable mixture; stir to combine well. Set aside.

5. Preheat oven to 200 degrees. Heat 1 tablespoon vegeta-

ble oil in large heavy-gauge skillet over medium heat until hot. Measure ¼ cup vegetable mixture, pour into skillet, and flatten with metal spatula into ¼-inch-thick pancake. Repeat with remaining vegetable mixture to make a total of 8 pancakes, frying as many at one time as will fit in skillet without crowding. Fry pancakes 2 to 3 minutes on each side, adding more oil as necessary. Transfer cooked pancakes to small baking sheet and keep warm in oven until ready to serve.

6. To serve, divide pancakes among 4 dinner plates and top with a dollop of yogurt sauce and a sprinkling of paprika.

Yogurt Sauce

Small clove garlic
½ cup low-fat plain yogurt
1 teaspoon Dijon mustard
Dash of hot pepper sauce
Pinch of sugar
Pinch of paprika

1. Peel and mince garlic.

2. Place all ingredients in small bowl and stir until well combined. Cover bowl and refrigerate until ready to serve.

Steamed Broccoli with Slivered Almonds

¾ pound broccoli
Large lemon
3 tablespoons Oriental sesame oil
Salt
Freshly ground pepper
½ cup slivered almonds

1. Wash broccoli and dry with paper towels. Cut tops into 2-inch florets; reserve remaining broccoli for another use. Halve lemon and squeeze enough juice to measure 3 tablespoons.

2. For dressing, combine lemon juice, sesame oil, and salt and pepper to taste in small bowl; set aside.

3. Over medium heat, bring 1 inch water to a boil in large saucepan fitted with vegetable steamer.

4. Place broccoli in steamer, cover pan, and cook 5 minutes, or until broccoli is crisp-tender.

5. Drain broccoli and transfer to large bowl. Add dressing and toss well. Divide broccoli among 4 dinner plates and sprinkle with slivered almonds.

Vicki Poth

A vegetarian since her teens, Vicki Poth realizes that meatless meals are usually thought of as being heavy and unappetizing, in part because they often rely on such filling foods as cheese, rice, and beans. Here she presents three menus that are light and elegant, and that will satisfy the appetites of vegetarians and meat-eaters alike.

The nutburgers of Menu 1 are the perfect solution for the hamburger-lover who has given up meat. The patties, made with ground nuts, seeds, *couscous*, and a spicy sauce, are browned and then served in pita bread. Instead of providing the usual sliced onion and tomato accompaniments, the cook serves the burgers with fresh coriander *salsa*. A sauté of red cabbage and carrot strips (a warmed version of coleslaw but without the rich mayonnaise dressing) adds color and additional texture to the meal.

Menu 2 is a meatless version of the American standby chicken pot pie. The cook captures the traditional richness of this dish without using cream and butter. Instead, she creates a sauce from seasoned tofu and yogurt, then mixes it with three different vegetables for the filling. For an elegant touch, the pie crust is made with puff pastry. Corn fritters layered with slices of goat cheese are the unusual side dish.

Vicki Poth offers her own adaptations of some Greek dishes in Menu 3. She enhances the *bryami*, or mixed vegetable casserole, with lots of fresh dill and a surprising touch of vinegar, and roasts sweet potatoes instead of white potatoes as the accompaniment. The tossed salad sprinkled with walnuts can be served before, with, or after the entrée.

Stuff the spicy nutburger, topped with Mexican-style sauce, into a pita for a delicious sandwich. The colorful warm salad contains red cabbage, carrots, and, for a touch of sweetness, grated apple.

Nutburgers with Fresh Coriander Salsa
Cabbage, Carrot, and Apple Sauté

The spicy nutburgers contain *couscous*, sunflower seeds, almonds, and peanuts. Made from finely ground semolina wheat, pellet-shaped *couscous* is sold in Middle Eastern markets, some supermarkets, and health food stores. If you wish, you may substitute bulgur wheat. For additional flavor, add two tablespoons of chopped fresh coriander to the uncooked nutburger mixture before sautéing. The nutburgers can be prepared a day in advance and refrigerated wrapped individually in foil. Allow them to come to room temperature before cooking. For a more piquant sauce, add a small *jalapeño* chili, finely minced, to the other ingredients.

WHAT TO DRINK

The cook recommends ice-cold sparkling cider to accompany this menu; cold dark beer would also complement the flavors of these dishes.

SHOPPING LIST AND STAPLES

Small head red cabbage
2 medium-size ripe tomatoes (about 1 pound total weight)
Large carrot
Small cucumber
Small green bell pepper
Small bunch scallions
2 small onions (about ½ pound total weight)
Large clove garlic
Small bunch coriander
Medium-size Granny Smith or Golden Delicious apple
Medium-size lemon
1 tablespoon vegetable oil
2 tablespoons apple cider vinegar, approximately
1 tablespoon Worcestershire sauce
¼ cup ketchup
4 medium-size whole-wheat or sesame pita breads
1-pound package couscous
1 teaspoon brown sugar
⅔ cup whole natural almonds
⅔ cup unsalted shelled raw or roasted peanuts
⅔ cup unsalted shelled raw sunflower seeds
1 tablespoon chili powder
1 teaspoon dry mustard
1 teaspoon ground cumin
½ teaspoon caraway seeds
¼ teaspoon ground coriander

¼ teaspoon Cayenne pepper
Salt
Freshly ground pepper

UTENSILS

Food processor or blender
Large nonstick skillet with cover
Large bowl
2 medium-size bowls, 1 nonaluminum
2 small nonaluminum bowls
Measuring cups and spoons
Chef's knife
Paring knife
2 wooden spoons
Rubber spatula
Nylon spatula
Grater
Citrus juicer (optional)
Vegetable peeler (optional)
Garlic press (optional)

START-TO-FINISH STEPS

1. Peel onions. Finely chop enough onion to measure ¼ cup for nutburgers recipe and coarsely chop enough onion to measure ½ cup for salsa recipe.
2. Follow nutburgers recipe steps 1 through 7.
3. Follow salsa recipe steps 1 through 3.
4. Follow sauté recipe steps 1 through 4.
5. Follow nutburgers recipe steps 8 and 9.
6. Follow sauté recipe steps 5 through 7, nutburgers recipe step 10, and serve.

RECIPES

Nutburgers with Fresh Coriander Salsa

¼ cup couscous
¼ cup ketchup
1 tablespoon Worcestershire sauce
1 tablespoon apple cider vinegar
1 tablespoon chili powder
1 teaspoon dry mustard
1 teaspoon ground cumin
1 teaspoon brown sugar
¼ teaspoon Cayenne pepper

¼ teaspoon ground coriander
Large clove garlic
Small green bell pepper
¼ cup finely chopped onion
⅔ cup whole natural almonds
⅔ cup unsalted shelled raw or roasted peanuts
⅔ cup unsalted shelled raw sunflower seeds
4 medium-size whole-wheat or sesame pita breads
Fresh Coriander Salsa (see following recipe)

1. Place couscous in large bowl and pour ¼ cup hot water over it. Cover bowl with plate and set aside 10 minutes, or until water is completely absorbed.
2. Meanwhile, in small nonaluminum bowl, combine ketchup, Worcestershire sauce, vinegar, chili powder, mustard, cumin, sugar, Cayenne, and coriander. Peel garlic. Using garlic press or flat blade of chef's knife, crush garlic and add to ketchup mixture.
3. Wash bell pepper and dry with paper towel. Halve, core, and seed pepper. Finely chop enough pepper to measure ¼ cup. Add pepper and onion to sauce, stirring until well combined. (The sauce will be very hot, but the flavors will mellow when combined with the nuts.)
4. Place almonds in food processor or blender and chop coarsely. Add peanuts and process 30 seconds to 1 minute, or until mixture gathers into a doughlike ball. Do not overprocess.
5. Add sunflower seeds and process another 30 seconds, or until seeds are coarsely chopped.
6. Turn nut mixture into bowl with couscous. Add ketchup mixture and stir until thoroughly combined. Mixture will be heavy. You should have about 2 cups.
7. To make each burger, pack mixture into ½-cup measuring cup. Turn onto large piece of waxed paper and repeat to make 4 nutburgers. Place another sheet of waxed paper over burgers and, using your hands, flatten burgers into patties about 3½ inches in diameter. Line platter with double thickness of paper towels.
8. Heat large nonstick skillet over medium heat. Place burgers in pan, cover, and cook 30 seconds to 1 minute, or until browned on one side. Turn burgers with spatula, cover skillet, and cook another 2 to 3 minutes, or until other side is lightly browned.
9. Remove burgers to paper-towel-lined platter to drain, cover loosely with foil, and keep warm on stove top until ready to serve.
10. To serve, place a nutburger and a pita bread on each of 4 dinner plates. Top each burger with some fresh coriander salsa and serve remaining salsa separately.

Fresh Coriander Salsa

2 medium-size ripe tomatoes (about 1 pound total weight)
Small cucumber
½ cup coarsely chopped onion
Small bunch coriander
Salt and freshly ground pepper
1 tablespoon apple cider vinegar, approximately

1. Wash tomatoes and dry with paper towels. Halve, core, and seed tomatoes, and coarsely chop enough to measure 2 cups. Turn tomatoes into medium-size nonaluminum bowl.
2. Halve cucumber lengthwise; do not peel. Using teaspoon, carefully remove seeds. Coarsely chop enough cucumber to measure ½ cup. Add cucumber and onion to tomatoes.

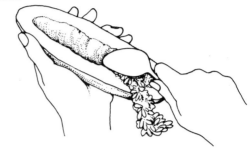

Use teaspoon to remove cucumber seeds.

3. Wash coriander and pat dry. Coarsely chop enough leaves to measure ⅓ cup, or more to taste. Add to other ingredients in bowl and toss gently. Season to taste with salt, pepper, and a few splashes of vinegar. Turn salsa into serving bowl or 4 individual bowls and set aside until needed.

Cabbage, Carrot, and Apple Sauté

Small head red cabbage
Large carrot
Medium-size lemon
Medium-size Granny Smith or Golden Delicious apple
2 to 4 medium-size scallions
1 tablespoon vegetable oil
½ teaspoon caraway seeds
Salt and freshly ground pepper

1. Wash, dry, quarter, and core cabbage. In food processor fitted with slicing disc, or with chef's knife, shred enough cabbage to measure 2 cups; reserve remainder for another use. Transfer cabbage to medium-size bowl.
2. Peel and trim carrot. Using food processor or coarse side of grater, grate carrot. Add carrot to cabbage.
3. Halve lemon and squeeze enough juice into small nonaluminum bowl to measure 2 tablespoons. Wash, halve, and core apple; do not peel. Using coarse side of grater, grate apple lengthwise. Add apple to lemon juice and toss; set aside.
4. Wash and trim scallions. Thinly slice enough white and green parts of scallions to measure ½ cup; set aside.
5. In large nonstick skillet, heat oil over medium heat until a piece of cabbage dropped into skillet sizzles. Add remaining cabbage and carrot. Sauté vegetables, stirring, 2 to 3 minutes, or until crisp-tender.
6. Add apple, scallions, and caraway seeds, and sauté, stirring, 1 minute, or just until apple and scallions are warmed through.
7. Remove skillet from heat. Season mixture to taste with salt and pepper and divide among 4 dinner plates.

Vegetable Pot Pie
Corn Fritters with Red Pepper Purée

In this country-style meal golden puff pastry tops a vegetable pot pie of cauliflower, carrots, and peas, and sliced goat cheese is layered with corn fritters napped with red pepper purée. Serve extra purée in a small pitcher.

The commercially prepared puff pastry used for the crust on the pot pie is easy to work with. It looks especially elegant with some pastry hearts, leaves, or shapes of your own design added on top. Brush the crust with lightly beaten egg yolk, then arrange your cut-out designs around the circumference of the pastry (designs placed over the center will lengthen the baking time). Brush the cut-outs with egg. For a slightly different flavor, the pot pie could be made with a combination of cauliflower and broccoli, or broccoli alone. If time permits, substitute whole finger carrots for the carrot slices and fresh peas for the frozen.

To vary the fritters recipe, select a goat cheese coated with herbs, or substitute warm applesauce for the red pepper purée.

WHAT TO DRINK

A crisp, acidic white wine such as California Sauvignon Blanc (sometimes labeled Fumé Blanc) would be good with this meal.

SHOPPING LIST AND STAPLES

½ pound firm tofu
Small head cauliflower
2 medium-size red bell peppers (about ½ pound total weight)
Large carrot
Medium-size red onion
Medium-size clove garlic
Medium-size lemon
3 eggs
¼ cup milk, approximately
½ pint plain yogurt
3 tablespoons lightly salted butter
¼-pound log chèvre
2 ounces Parmesan cheese
1-pound package frozen puff pastry
10-ounce package frozen corn kernels
10-ounce package frozen peas
1 tablespoon good-quality olive oil
1 tablespoon whole-grain Dijon mustard
1 teaspoon Worcestershire sauce
Hot pepper sauce
½ cup all-purpose flour

1 teaspoon baking powder
¼ teaspoon ground nutmeg
Salt and freshly ground pepper

UTENSILS

Food processor or blender
2 large heavy-gauge skillets with covers
2-quart soufflé dish or 6½-inch round baking dish
Large baking sheet
Large ovenproof serving platter
3 large bowls
2 small bowls
Colander
Measuring cups and spoons
Chef's knife
Paring knife
2 wooden spoons
Metal spatula
Rubber spatula
Rolling pin
Grater
Whisk
Pastry brush
Small leaf- or heart-shaped cookie cutter (optional)

START-TO-FINISH STEPS

1. Follow pot pie recipe steps 1 through 10.
2. While pot pie is baking, follow fritters recipe steps 1 and 2 and purée recipe steps 1 through 5.
3. Follow fritters recipe steps 3 through 5.
4. Follow purée recipe step 6 if necessary.
5. Follow fritters recipe steps 6 and 7, pot pie recipe step 11, and serve.

RECIPES

Vegetable Pot Pie

1-pound package frozen puff pastry
½ pound firm tofu
Small head cauliflower
Large carrot
Medium-size clove garlic
2 ounces Parmesan cheese
¼ cup plain yogurt
1 tablespoon whole-grain Dijon mustard

1 teaspoon Worcestershire sauce
¼ teaspoon ground nutmeg
¼ teaspoon freshly ground pepper
Salt
10-ounce package frozen peas
1 egg

1. Preheat oven to 425 degrees.
2. Remove puff pastry from freezer and let thaw in original wrapper 15 minutes, or until pastry can be cut with sharp knife but is still cold to touch.
3. Meanwhile, if tofu is packed in water, drain in colander; remove to plate and set aside.
4. In large heavy-gauge skillet, bring 1 cup water to a boil over high heat. Meanwhile, wash cauliflower and carrot and dry with paper towels. Trim and discard stem and leaves from cauliflower and cut enough cauliflower into bite-size florets to measure about 3 cups. Peel, trim, and cut carrot crosswise into ¼-inch-thick slices. Add cauliflower and carrot to boiling water and reduce heat to medium. Cover pan and simmer vegetables 8 to 10 minutes, or until tender.
5. Meanwhile, blot tofu dry with paper towels and crumble into container of food processor or blender. Peel and quarter garlic. Using grater, finely grate enough Parmesan to measure ½ cup. Add Parmesan to tofu along with garlic, yogurt, mustard, Worcestershire sauce, nutmeg, pepper, and a pinch of salt. Process 30 seconds, or until mixture is smooth and creamy, scraping down sides of container if necessary. Adjust seasonings to taste and reserve mixture in container.
6. Unwrap puff pastry and unfold on cutting board. Roll out pastry into 8 by 11-inch sheet. Invert 2-quart soufflé dish or 6½-inch round baking dish on top of pastry. Using a sharp knife, and using the rim of the dish as a guide, cut a pastry round 1 inch larger than dish. Using sharp knife or a small cookie cutter, cut 3 or 4 leaf- or heart-shaped designs, or designs of your own, from remaining pastry. Place the cutting board with the puff pastry and cut-out designs on it in freezer while assembling vegetables and sauce. Grease soufflé or baking dish.
7. Turn cooked vegetables into colander and add ¼ cup frozen peas to colander. Return remaining peas to freezer for another use. Shake colander to drain vegetables well. Turn vegetables into large bowl, add tofu sauce, and toss gently to coat vegetables evenly. Turn vegetables and sauce into prepared dish.

8. Remove pastry from freezer; set aside cut-outs. Carefully invert pastry round over soufflé or baking dish, resting it on rim of dish so it does not touch filling. There should be about 1 inch of space between vegetables and pastry. Press overlapping edge of pastry against exterior of dish.

9. Separate egg and place yolk in small bowl; reserve white for another use. Lightly beat egg yolk. Using pastry brush, lightly brush top of pastry with a thin coating of egg yolk. If edges of pastry do not adhere to sides of dish, use egg yolk to "glue" crust in place. Gently arrange cut-out designs around circumference of top pastry. Lightly brush design with egg yolk.

10. Bake pie 25 to 30 minutes, or until pastry is puffed and golden brown.

11. To serve, cut pastry crust into wedges, place on dinner plates, and spoon filling on top of crust.

Corn Fritters with Red Pepper Purée

10-ounce package frozen corn kernels
¼-pound log chèvre, well chilled
2 eggs
2 to 4 tablespoons milk
½ cup all-purpose flour
1 teaspoon baking powder
½ teaspoon salt
¼ teaspoon freshly ground pepper
3 tablespoons lightly salted butter
Red Pepper Purée (see following recipe)

1. Place 1½ cups frozen corn kernels in colander and separate kernels with fork; set aside. Return remaining corn to freezer for another use.

2. Cut chèvre into eight ¼-inch-thick rounds, wiping knife with damp paper towel after cutting each slice. Place slices on small plate. Lightly cover plate with plastic wrap and set aside.

3. In large bowl, lightly whisk together eggs and 2 tablespoons milk. In small bowl, combine flour, baking powder, salt, and pepper. Gradually whisk dry ingredients into egg mixture, and continue whisking just until batter is smooth.

4. Separate any corn kernels that may still be stuck together and shake colander to remove excess moisture. Stir corn into batter. If batter is too thick, stir in additional milk, 1 teaspoon at a time, until batter drops slowly from spoon.

5. Line large baking sheet with paper towels. In large heavy-gauge skillet, melt 1 tablespoon butter over medium heat. When butter is hot and bubbly, drop batter by tablespoonsful into skillet; you should be able to fry about 5 or 6 fritters at once. Fry fritters 1½ minutes on one side, or until edges begin to brown and bubbles appear on top. Using metal spatula, turn fritters and cook 1½ minutes on other side, or until golden. Transfer first batch of cooked fritters to paper-towel-lined baking sheet and cover loosely with foil; keep warm on stove top. Remove skillet from heat and wipe out with paper towels. Add more butter and repeat process for remaining batter.

6. Using some of red pepper purée, make a 1-inch border around outside of large ovenproof serving platter. Turn remaining purée into small pitcher. Overlap fritters on top of purée and place chèvre slices between fritters.

7. Place platter in 425-degree oven 2 to 3 minutes to reheat fritters. Serve with remaining purée.

Red Pepper Purée

1 tablespoon good-quality olive oil
Medium-size red onion
2 medium-size red bell peppers (about ½ pound total weight)
Medium-size lemon
Salt and freshly ground pepper
Hot pepper sauce

1. In large skillet, heat oil over medium-high heat. Meanwhile, peel and coarsely chop onion. Place a piece of onion in skillet. When it sizzles, add remaining onion and sauté 1 to 2 minutes, or until soft.

2. While onion is cooking, wash, halve, core, and seed peppers. Coarsely chop peppers and add to skillet.

3. Halve lemon and squeeze enough juice to measure 2 tablespoons. Add juice to skillet and stir until mixture simmers. Cover and simmer 10 minutes, or until peppers are tender. (Vegetables should be simmering during entire cooking period. If not, adjust heat.)

4. Turn mixture and cooking liquid into container of food processor or blender. Purée, scraping down sides of container as necessary, 30 seconds, or until mixture is thick.

5. Return purée to skillet and season to taste with salt, pepper, and hot pepper sauce. Remove pan from heat, cover, and set aside on stove top until needed.

6. Just before serving, check purée to see if it has cooled. If so, reheat, covered, over low heat.

Bryami with Feta-Yogurt Sauce
Roasted Sweet Potatoes
Mixed Salad with Walnut Vinaigrette

A Greek vegetable casserole topped with feta-yogurt sauce makes an appetizing partner for roasted sweet potatoes and a tossed salad.

Garlicky feta-yogurt sauce is a perfect complement to the *bryami*. Feta, a Greek goat's milk cheese, has a soft, crumbly texture and a tangy flavor. Because it is preserved in brine, feta may be quite salty; you may want to rinse it before using it in the recipe. Let its saltiness dictate whether you need to add salt to the sauce or the casserole. Feta is sold packaged and by weight in cheese shops and many supermarkets.

The salad contains two Italian vegetables, radicchio and fennel. A relative of chicory with deep purple to light red leaves, radicchio is prized as a salad vegetable for its pleasantly bitter flavor. It is available in fall and winter,

and should be stored as you would lettuce. Fennel, also know as *finocchio*, resembles a flattened bunch of celery with a bulbous base, long white stalks, and feathery green leaves. It has a faint yet distinctive taste of licorice. This late fall to early spring vegetable can be refrigerated for up to five days. Select firm, unblemished bulbs.

WHAT TO DRINK

A traditional match for this Greek-inspired menu is Retsina, a popular Greek table wine. If it is not available, select an Italian Verdicchio or a young Barbera.

SHOPPING LIST AND STAPLES

6 to 8 medium-size ripe plum tomatoes, or 2 large ripe
  tomatoes (about 1½ pounds total weight)
Medium-size eggplant (about 1 pound)
4 medium-size sweet potatoes (about 2 pounds total
  weight)
3 small zucchini (about 1 pound total weight)
Medium-size head Boston or Bibb lettuce
Medium-size head radicchio
Medium-size fennel bulb
Medium-size onion
Medium-size clove garlic
Small bunch dill
1 pint plain yogurt
2 tablespoons lightly salted butter
½ pound feta cheese
¼ cup good-quality olive oil
¼ cup walnut oil
¼ cup red wine vinegar
2 teaspoons whole-grain Dijon mustard
1 ounce walnut pieces (about 3 tablespoons)
Salt
Freshly ground pepper

UTENSILS

Large stockpot with cover
17 x 11-inch jelly-roll pan
2-quart casserole
Small baking dish
2 medium-size bowls
Colander
Salad spinner (optional)
Measuring cups and spoons
Chef's knife
Paring knife
Rubber spatula
Small jar with tight-fitting lid
Garlic press (optional)
Kitchen shears (optional)

START-TO-FINISH STEPS

1. Follow bryami recipe step 1 and sweet potatoes recipe
step 1.
2. Follow bryami recipe steps 2 through 5 and sweet potatoes recipe step 2.
3. While sweet potatoes are cooking, follow bryami recipe
steps 6 and 7.
4. Follow sweet potatoes recipe steps 3 through 6.
5. While bryami and sweet potatoes are baking, follow
salad recipe steps 1 through 5 and sauce recipe steps 1
and 2.
6. Follow bryami recipe step 8 and salad recipe steps 6
and 7.
7. Follow sweet potatoes recipe steps 7 and 8, bryami
recipe step 9, and serve with salad.

RECIPES

Bryami with Feta-Yogurt Sauce

Medium-size eggplant (about 1 pound)
3 small zucchini (about 1 pound total weight)
6 to 8 medium-size ripe plum tomatoes, or 2 large ripe
  tomatoes (about 1½ pounds total weight)
Small bunch dill
Medium-size onion
¼ cup good-quality olive oil
2 tablespoons red wine vinegar
¼ teaspoon freshly ground pepper
Feta-Yogurt Sauce (see following recipe)

1. Preheat oven to 400 degrees.
2. Wash eggplant, zucchini, tomatoes, and dill, and dry
with paper towels. Trim stem ends of eggplant and zucchini. Core tomatoes. Peel and halve onion.
3. Halve eggplant lengthwise, and cut each half crosswise
into ¼-inch-thick slices; you should have about 4 cups. Set
aside. Cut zucchini crosswise into ¼-inch-thick slices; set
aside. Thinly slice onion. Cut tomatoes crosswise into ¼-
inch-thick slices.
4. Using kitchen shears or sharp paring knife, trim dill
sprigs from stems. Reserve 4 sprigs for garnish. Coarsely
chop enough remaining sprigs to measure about 1 cup
loosely packed.
5. In small jar with tight-fitting lid, combine oil, vinegar,
and pepper. Shake until well blended. Sprinkle 1 tablespoon dressing on bottom of 2-quart casserole.
6. Overlap half of eggplant slices in casserole. Top with
half of zucchini slices, followed by half of onion and tomato
slices. Sprinkle with ½ cup chopped dill and 2½ tablespoons dressing. Repeat layering process until all ingredients are used.
7. Bake bryami, uncovered, 30 minutes, or until vegetables are tender when pierced with tip of knife.
8. Remove casserole from oven, cover with foil, and set
aside on stove top until ready to serve.
9. To serve, divide bryami among 4 dinner plates and
spoon some feta-yogurt sauce on top. Garnish each portion
with a dill sprig.

Feta-Yogurt Sauce

½ pound feta cheese
1 pint plain yogurt
⅛ teaspoon freshly ground pepper
Medium-size clove garlic
Salt (optional)

1. Taste feta cheese for saltiness and rinse under cold
running water, if desired; pat dry. Coarsely crumble feta
into medium-size bowl. Add yogurt and pepper.
2. Peel garlic. Using garlic press or flat blade of chef's
knife, crush garlic and add to bowl. Stir mixture until well
combined and season with salt to taste if desired. Set
sauce aside until needed.

Roasted Sweet Potatoes

4 medium-size sweet potatoes (about 2 pounds total
  weight)
2 tablespoons lightly salted butter

1. In large stockpot, bring enough water to cover sweet potatoes to a boil over high heat. Wash potatoes and trim ends. Do not peel.
2. Place potatoes in boiling water, reduce heat to medium-high, cover, and cook 10 minutes.
3. Drain potatoes in colander and set aside to cool at least 5 minutes.
4. Meanwhile, melt butter in 17 by 11-inch jelly-roll pan in preheated 400-degree oven about 1 minute. Remove pan from oven and set aside.
5. Halve potatoes lengthwise. Place each half, cut-side down, on cutting surface and slice lengthwise into ½-inch-wide strips. Arrange sliced potatoes in single layer in jelly-roll pan.
6. Bake potatoes in 400-degree oven 20 minutes, or until tender when pierced with tip of sharp knife.
7. After 20 minutes, increase oven temperature to broil or turn on broiler. Broil potatoes about 3 inches from heat 30 to 60 seconds, or just until well browned and crisp on outside.
8. Divide potatoes among 4 dinner plates and serve.

Mixed Salad with Walnut Vinaigrette

1 ounce walnut pieces (about 3 tablespoons)
Medium-size fennel bulb
Medium-size head Boston or Bibb lettuce
Medium-size head radicchio
¼ cup walnut oil
2 tablespoons red wine vinegar
2 teaspoons whole-grain Dijon mustard
Salt and freshly ground pepper

1. Place walnuts in small baking dish and toast in preheated 400-degree oven, stirring occasionally, 4 to 5 minutes, or until lightly browned and crisp.
2. Meanwhile, using paring knife, remove and discard tough outer stalks from fennel. Wash, dry, and core bulb. Wash lettuce and radicchio and separate into leaves; dry in salad spinner or with paper towels.

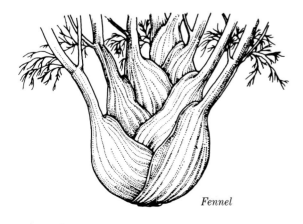

Fennel

3. Remove walnuts from oven and set aside to cool.
4. Wrap lettuce and radicchio in kitchen towel and refrigerate until needed. Place fennel in plastic bag and refrigerate until needed.
5. In small jar with tight-fitting lid, combine walnut oil, wine, vinegar, and mustard. Shake until well combined; season to taste with salt and pepper. Set dressing aside until needed.
6. Just before serving, line 4 salad plates with lettuce and radicchio leaves. Tear remaining leaves into bite-size pieces and place in medium-size bowl. Thinly slice fennel and add to bowl.
7. Shake vinaigrette to recombine. Pour about half of vinaigrette into bowl, and toss to coat salad. If necessary, add more vinaigrette. Divide greens among salad plates and sprinkle each salad with some toasted walnuts. Serve any remaining dressing separately.

ADDED TOUCH

To vary this nutritious dessert, halve the number of figs and dates and add some pitted prunes and dried apricot halves. You can also use chopped walnuts in place of some of the coconut.

Fruit and Coconut Slices

10 dried Calimyrna figs
12 whole pitted dried dates
1 tablespoon honey
Pinch of cinnamon
1 cup sweetened or unsweetened flaked coconut
Medium-size orange

1. Remove stems from figs. Quarter figs. In food processor or blender, combine figs, dates, honey, and cinnamon. Process 1 to 2 minutes, or until fruit is coarsely chopped.
2. Add coconut and process another 30 seconds, or until mixture resembles coarse meal.
3. Turn mixture onto a large piece of waxed paper. Wrap the waxed paper around the mixture and roll into a 1-inch log about 10 inches long. Tightly wrap mixture in same waxed paper, place in plastic bag, and refrigerate at least 15 minutes, or until firm.
4. Meanwhile, wash and dry orange and cut crosswise into thin slices.
5. Cut chilled fruit log crosswise into ½-inch-thick slices. Divide orange slices among 4 dessert plates and top with slices of fruit log.

LEFTOVER SUGGESTION

Leftover *bryami* and feta-yogurt sauce can be used as the filling for an omelet or the topping for whole-grain pasta, *couscous*, brown rice, or bulgur or cracked wheat. Or, serve *bryami* at room temperature in a pita pocket and top it with the feta-yogurt sauce. By itself, the sauce makes an excellent dip for crudités or a spread for toasted whole-grain bread.

Barbara Chernetz

According to Barbara Chernetz, a strong interest in health and fitness (and a passion for Mexican foods) influences her menu planning. Although she believes in adhering to time-honored cooking traditions when preparing ethnic foods, she also likes to experiment with recipes, using whatever fresh ingredients are in season. Many of her meatless dishes incorporate dairy products because they are good sources of protein.

In Menu 3, she offers a cold spicy walnut sauce spooned over hot vermicelli, a pasta frequently eaten in Mexico. For extra protein, Barbara Chernetz adds ricotta cheese to the sauce. The salad is an interesting mix of sliced jícama and fruit.

Menus 1 and 2 show just how vibrant vegetarian food can be. Perfect for a festive occasion, Menu 1 features *enchiladas* (filled tortillas) and cumin rice as the main course. The *enchiladas* are filled with cheese, baked with a piquant tomato sauce, and then garnished with sour cream and slices of lime and olives. A colorful tomatillo and plum tomato salad introduces the meal.

The focus of Menu 2 is a bright green, red, and yellow vegetable hash *(salpicón de legumbres)*. Guests spoon the hash onto warm flour tortillas, add spicy salsa, then roll up the tortillas. The accompanying pinto bean dip can be offered as an appetizer, if you prefer.

A gaily appointed table befits this lavish Mexican meal. Offer each guest enchiladas *and a generous serving of rice and, for added visual appeal, garnish each plate with shredded lettuce, radish slices, and a wedge of avocado. Serve the tomatillo, tomato, and onion salad before or with the main course.*

Cheese Enchiladas
Cumin Rice
Tomatillo Salad

Two cheeses—semi-soft Monterey Jack, which melts well, and crumbly *queso fresco*, a fresh, unaged Mexican cheese—are combined in the *enchiladas*. If you cannot find *queso fresco*, substitute a moist farmer cheese.

The delicately seasoned rice calls for *pepitas*, or pumpkin seeds. Buy unsalted seeds and refrigerate them in a tightly closed jar or plastic bag. Look for *pepitas* in health food or specialty food stores.

Fresh tomatillos are a primary ingredient in the bright salad. Also called *tomates verdes*, tomatillos have a brown papery husk that must be removed before cooking. Once the husk is removed, tomatillos resemble small green tomatoes. Buy fresh tomatillos in supermarkets or Mexican groceries, selecting those that are green to yellow-green in color, plump, and firm. Store them unwashed in a paper bag in your refrigerator for up to three weeks. Canned tomatillos, sold in the Mexican food section of many supermarkets, may be substituted if fresh are unavailable.

WHAT TO DRINK

To accompany these delicately spicy dishes the cook suggests a sangría punch made with white wine (preferably a Spanish white Rioja), sliced fresh fruit, and soda water.

SHOPPING LIST AND STAPLES

Small head iceberg lettuce (optional)
Large bunch red radishes
½ pound fresh tomatillos, or 13-ounce can tomatillos
½ pound plum tomatoes
Medium-size red onion
Small bunch coriander
Small avocado (optional)
Large lime
½ pint sour cream
1 tablespoon unsalted butter
¾ pound Monterey Jack or white Cheddar cheese
10 ounces queso fresco or farmer cheese
12 fresh corn tortillas, 7 to 8 inches in diameter
6-ounce can pitted black olives
10-ounce can mild or hot red enchilada sauce or chili sauce
¼ cup good-quality olive oil
¼ cup plus 2 teaspoons vegetable oil
1 tablespoon red wine vinegar
1 cup long-grain white rice

5 tablespoons hulled pumpkin seeds (about 1½ ounces)
2 teaspoons ground cumin, approximately
Salt and freshly ground pepper

UTENSILS

Food processor (optional)
Small skillet
Medium-size skillet
Medium-size saucepan with cover
13 x 9-inch baking pan
2 medium-size bowls
Small bowl
Strainer
Measuring cups and spoons
Chef's knife
Paring knife
Wooden spoon
Slotted spoon
Metal spatula
Grater (if not using food processor)
Whisk
Metal tongs

START-TO-FINISH STEPS

1. Wash radishes and coriander and dry with paper towels. Slice 2 radishes, if using, for enchiladas recipe. Slice enough remaining radishes to measure ¾ cup for salad recipe. Mince enough coriander to measure 2 tablespoons for rice recipe and 1 tablespoon for salad recipe.
2. Follow enchiladas recipe steps 1 through 3.
3. Follow rice recipe step 1.
4. While rice is cooking, follow enchiladas recipe steps 4 through 6.
5. Follow rice recipe steps 2 and 3 and salad recipe steps 1 through 4.
6. Follow enchiladas recipe step 7 and salad recipe step 5.
7. Follow enchiladas recipe step 8, rice recipe step 4, and serve with salad.

RECIPES

Cheese Enchiladas

¾ pound Monterey Jack or white Cheddar cheese
10 ounces queso fresco or farmer cheese
6-ounce can pitted black olives

Large lime
Small head iceberg lettuce (optional)
¼ cup vegetable oil
12 fresh corn tortillas, 7 to 8 inches in diameter
Salt and freshly ground pepper
1 cup mild or hot red enchilada sauce or chili sauce
Small avocado (optional)
½ cup sour cream
2 radishes, sliced (optional)

1. Preheat oven to 350 degrees.
2. Using food processor or grater, grate enough Monterey Jack or Cheddar cheese to measure about 3 cups. Crumble enough queso fresco or farmer cheese to measure about 2½ cups. Drain olives in strainer. Thinly slice 4 olives and set aside for garnish. Coarsely chop enough remaining olives to measure ¾ cup; set aside.
3. Wash lime, and lettuce if using, and dry with paper towels. Shred enough lettuce to measure 1 cup. Thinly slice lime; set aside.
4. Heat 2 tablespoons oil in medium-size skillet over medium heat until surface ripples. Place 1 tortilla in oil and cook 2 to 3 seconds, or just until softened and pliable. Turn with tongs and cook another 2 to 3 seconds. Transfer tortilla to plate. Cook remaining tortillas in same manner, adding remaining 2 tablespoons oil as needed. Stack tortillas, cover with foil, and keep warm on stove top until needed.
5. Combine 1½ cups grated Monterey Jack or Cheddar, all of queso fresco or farmer cheese, chopped olives, and salt and pepper to taste in medium-size bowl and stir to blend. Place about ⅓ cup of cheese mixture on each tortilla. Roll up tortillas and place, seam-side down, in ungreased 13 by 9-inch baking pan. Pour enchilada sauce over enchiladas and sprinkle with remaining Monterey Jack.
6. Cover pan with foil and bake enchiladas 20 minutes, or until heated through.
7. Just before serving, halve avocado, if using. Peel and thinly slice one half. Reserve remaining half for another use.
8. Using metal spatula, transfer enchiladas to 4 dinner plates. Garnish each serving with lime slices, dollop of sour cream, and sliced olives. Serve with shredded lettuce, radish slices, and avocado slices, if desired.

Cumin Rice

1 cup long-grain white rice
1 tablespoon unsalted butter
1½ to 2 teaspoons ground cumin
½ teaspoon salt
2 teaspoons vegetable oil
5 tablespoons hulled pumpkin seeds (about 1½ ounces)
2 tablespoons minced coriander

1. Combine rice, 2 cups water, butter, cumin, and salt in medium-size saucepan and bring to a boil over medium-high heat. Reduce heat to low and simmer, covered, 15 minutes, or until rice is tender.
2. Line plate with paper towel. Heat oil in small skillet over medium-low heat until hot. Add pumpkin seeds and cook, shaking skillet frequently, 3 to 4 minutes, or until lightly browned. Using slotted spoon, transfer seeds to paper-towel-lined plate to drain.
3. Remove rice from heat and allow to rest, covered, at least 10 minutes.
4. To serve, fluff rice with fork and stir in pumpkin seeds and coriander. Divide rice among 4 dinner plates.

Tomatillo Salad

½ pound fresh tomatillos, or 13-ounce can tomatillos
½ pound plum tomatoes
Medium-size red onion
¼ cup good-quality olive oil
¾ cup sliced red radishes
1 tablespoon red wine vinegar
1 tablespoon minced coriander
Salt and freshly ground pepper

1. If using fresh tomatillos, peel husks, wash off sticky residue, and cut tomatillos into ¼-inch-thick slices. Or, drain canned tomatillos in strainer.
2. Wash tomatoes and dry with paper towels. Cut crosswise into ¼-inch-thick slices. Peel and thinly slice onion.
3. If using fresh tomatillos, heat 1 tablespoon oil in small skillet over medium heat until hot. Reduce heat to low, add fresh tomatillo slices, and cook 1 to 2 minutes, or just until lightly browned. Turn slices and cook another 1 to 2 minutes, or until lightly browned.
4. Combine fresh or canned tomatillos, tomatoes, onion, and radishes in medium-size bowl, and set aside until ready to serve.
5. Just before serving, whisk together 3 tablespoons oil, vinegar, coriander, and salt and pepper to taste in small bowl until well combined. Pour over salad and toss. Divide salad among 4 small plates.

Spicy Bean Dip
Vegetable Hash with Salsa Rio Piña

This Mexican brunch or dinner features creamy bean dip and tortilla chips, vegetable hash with chunky salsa, and flour tortillas.

Winter and summer squash, available year round at most supermarkets, are both used in the quick vegetable hash. All squash should feel heavy for their size, but small zucchini tend to be more flavorful than large ones. Avoid squash that are soft or that have breaks in the skin. Store winter squash in a cool, dry, well-ventilated place for up to four weeks. Refrigerate zucchini in a plastic bag and use them within two weeks.

WHAT TO DRINK

Beer, particularly a full-bodied Mexican brand, would be the ideal choice here.

SHOPPING LIST AND STAPLES

1 small plus 2 medium-size tomatoes
½ pound winter squash, such as butternut, Hubbard, or pumpkin
½ pound zucchini
Large red bell pepper
Small yellow or green bell pepper
4 fresh jalapeño or serrano chilies, or 4-ounce can
Small bunch scallions
2 large onions
3 medium-size cloves garlic
Small bunch coriander
Medium-size lemon
½ pint heavy cream
½ pint sour cream
4 tablespoons unsalted butter
¼ pound Monterey Jack cheese
12 flour tortillas, 7 to 8 inches in diameter
10-ounce package frozen corn kernels
7½-ounce package tortilla chips
15½-ounce can pinto beans
2 tablespoons vegetable oil
½ teaspoon dried oregano
½ teaspoon ground cumin
¼ teaspoon Cayenne pepper
Salt and freshly ground black pepper

UTENSILS

Food processor or blender
9- to 10-inch flameproof skillet with cover
Medium-size skillet
Strainer
Measuring cups and spoons
Chef's knife
Paring knife
Wooden spoon
Rubber spatula
Grater (if not using food processor)
Thin rubber gloves

START-TO-FINISH STEPS

Thirty minutes ahead: Separate 1 cup frozen corn kernels and set out to thaw for hash recipe.

1. Wash and dry fresh chilies, if using. If using canned chilies, drain in strainer. Wearing rubber gloves, seed and chop chilies for hash, dip, and salsa recipes. Coarsely chop tomatoes for dip and salsa recipes. Peel and finely chop onions for dip and hash recipes. Peel and mince garlic for dip, hash, and salsa recipes.
2. Follow dip recipe steps 1 through 4.
3. Follow hash recipe steps 1 through 4.
4. While onion mixture is cooking, follow salsa recipe step 1.
5. Follow hash recipe steps 5 and 6 and salsa recipe step 2.
6. Follow hash recipe steps 7 through 11 and serve with dip and salsa.

RECIPES

Spicy Bean Dip

15½-ounce can pinto beans
2 tablespoons vegetable oil
1 cup finely chopped onion
1 tablespoon seeded and chopped fresh or canned chilies
2 teaspoons minced garlic
Small tomato, coarsely chopped
½ teaspoon salt
½ teaspoon ground cumin
¼ teaspoon Cayenne pepper
¼ cup sour cream
7½-ounce package tortilla chips

1. Drain pinto beans in strainer.
2. Heat oil in medium-size skillet over medium heat until surface ripples. Add onion, chilies, and garlic, and cook, stirring occasionally, 3 to 4 minutes, or until softened. Remove skillet from heat.
3. Combine pinto beans, onion mixture, tomato, salt, cumin, and Cayenne in container of food processor or blender and process until mixture is a thick purée. Add sour cream and process until smooth.
4. Transfer dip to serving bowl, place on platter with tortilla chips, and set aside until ready to serve.

Vegetable Hash with Salsa Rio Piña

½ pound winter squash, such as butternut, Hubbard, or pumpkin
½ pound zucchini
Large red bell pepper
¼ pound Monterey Jack cheese
4 tablespoons unsalted butter
1½ cups finely chopped onion
2 tablespoons seeded and chopped fresh or canned chilies
2 teaspoons minced garlic
1 cup frozen corn kernels, thawed
1 teaspoon salt
½ teaspoon dried oregano
¼ teaspoon freshly ground pepper
12 flour tortillas, 7 to 8 inches in diameter
3 tablespoons heavy cream
Salsa Rio Piña (see following recipe)

1. Peel winter squash. Wash and dry zucchini and bell pepper. Trim zucchini. Halve, core, and seed pepper. Cut vegetables into ½-inch dice; set aside.
2. Grate enough Monterey Jack to measure 1 cup.
3. Preheat oven to 350 degrees.
4. Melt butter in 9- to 10-inch flameproof skillet over medium heat. When foam subsides, add onion, chilies, and garlic, and cook 5 minutes, or until lightly browned.
5. Add diced vegetables, corn, and seasonings to skillet and cook, covered, over medium heat, 7 to 8 minutes.
6. Meanwhile, wrap tortillas in foil in stacks of three. Heat in oven 5 minutes.
7. Increase heat under skillet to medium-high and cook, uncovered, 3 to 4 minutes, or until liquid is absorbed.
8. Remove tortillas from oven; do not unwrap. Keep warm on stove top. Turn oven to broil, or preheat broiler.
9. Spoon cream around sides of skillet, 1 tablespoon at a time, and cook hash another 5 minutes, or until cream is absorbed and vegetables are lightly browned. Remove skillet from heat.
10. Sprinkle hash with grated cheese and broil 4 inches from heat 1 to 2 minutes, or until cheese is melted and lightly browned.
11. Serve hash with warm tortillas and Salsa Rio Piña.

Salsa Rio Piña

Small yellow or green bell pepper
2 to 3 scallions
Small bunch coriander
Medium-size lemon
2 medium-size tomatoes, coarsely chopped
1 tablespoon seeded and chopped fresh or canned chilies
½ teaspoon minced garlic

1. Wash and dry pepper, scallions, and coriander. Halve, core, seed, and coarsely chop pepper. Coarsely chop scallions. Finely chop enough coriander to measure 1 tablespoon. Squeeze enough lemon juice to measure 2 tablespoons.
2. Combine all ingredients with 2 tablespoons water in small serving bowl. Set salsa aside.

Vermicelli with Walnut Sauce
Tropical Salad
Mexican Hot Chocolate

The tropical salad includes jícama, mango, and avocado. Jícama is a crunchy tuber that resembles a turnip but tastes like a cross between an apple and a water chestnut. You can find whole or cut-up jícama in well-stocked supermarkets and in Latin-American groceries. Store whole jícama in the refrigerator in a plastic bag, and the cut-up tuber immersed in water in a covered container. If jícama is unavailable, substitute ½ pound Jerusalem artichokes. If mango is unavailable, substitute cantaloupe.

The Mexican hot chocolate, served for dessert here, calls for Mexican chocolate. Commercially packaged in round or square cakes, Mexican chocolate is sweetened and flavored with cinnamon, vanilla, and ground almonds. You can find it at Latin-American groceries and specialty food shops. For a satisfactory substitute, melt 1½ ounces of dark sweet chocolate with ¼ teaspoon of ground cinnamon and dashes of almond and vanilla extracts. You can eliminate the Kahlúa from the recipe if you are serving the hot chocolate to children.

WHAT TO DRINK

Serve a white wine such as a California Chardonnay, an Alsatian Pinot Blanc, or a northern Italian Pinot Bianco.

SHOPPING LIST AND STAPLES

½ pound jícama or Jerusalem artichokes
Small red bell pepper
Small bunch watercress
Small fresh jalapeño or serrano chili, or 4-ounce can
Medium-size onion
1 or 2 large cloves garlic
Small bunch coriander
Large mango or small cantaloupe (about 1 pound)
Large avocado
Large pink grapefruit
2 limes
1 quart milk
½ pint heavy cream
8-ounce container ricotta cheese
1 cup good-quality olive oil, approximately
1 teaspoon vanilla extract
1 pound vermicelli
1 cup walnut pieces
½ cup salted cashews
1½ ounces Mexican chocolate
6 tablespoons sugar

Vermicelli with walnut sauce, topped with diced red pepper and lime wedges, looks particularly dramatic on dark dinnerware. Accompany the pasta with a jícama and fruit salad and offer mugs of Mexican hot chocolate for dessert.

¼ cup unsweetened cocoa powder
Pinch of freshly grated nutmeg
4 cinnamon sticks
Salt and freshly ground pepper
2 to 3 tablespoons Kahlúa

UTENSILS

Food processor or blender
Small skillet
Large saucepan
Medium-size heavy-gauge saucepan
Jelly-roll pan
Medium-size nonaluminum bowl
Small bowl
Colander
Measuring cups and spoons
Chef's knife
Paring knife
Wooden spoon
Thin rubber gloves

START-TO-FINISH STEPS

1. Follow vermicelli recipe steps 1 through 7.
2. While water heats, follow salad recipe steps 1 through 4.
3. Follow vermicelli recipe steps 8 and 9 and salad recipe step 5.
4. Follow vermicelli recipe step 10 and serve with salad.
5. Follow hot chocolate recipe steps 1 and 2 and serve.

RECIPES

Vermicelli with Walnut Sauce

2 limes
Small red bell pepper
Small fresh or canned jalapeño or serrano chili
Medium-size onion
1 or 2 large cloves garlic
1 cup walnut pieces
⅓ to ½ cup good-quality olive oil
1 pound vermicelli
½ cup salted cashews
½ cup ricotta cheese
½ to ¾ cup heavy cream
½ teaspoon salt

1. Preheat oven to 350 degrees.
2. Wash and dry limes, bell pepper, and fresh chili if using. Drain canned chili, if using. Wearing rubber gloves, seed and finely chop enough chili to measure 1 tablespoon. Squeeze enough juice from 1 lime to measure 2 tablespoons. Cut remaining lime into thin wedges; set aside. Halve, core, seed, and dice bell pepper; set aside.
3. Peel and thinly slice onion. Peel and thinly slice garlic.
4. Place walnuts on jelly-roll pan and toast in oven, shaking pan occasionally, 8 to 10 minutes, or until golden.
5. Meanwhile, heat 1 tablespoon oil in small skillet over medium heat until surface ripples. Add chili, onion, and

garlic, and cook, stirring occasionally, 3 to 4 minutes, or until onion is slightly softened. Remove pan from heat.
6. Remove walnuts from oven and set aside to cool.
7. Bring 2 quarts water to a boil in large saucepan over high heat.
8. Add vermicelli to boiling water and cook according to package directions until *al dente*.
9. Meanwhile, place nuts in container of food processor or blender and grind finely. Add onion mixture, ricotta, ½ cup cream, ⅓ cup olive oil, lime juice, and salt, and process to a thick purée. For a thinner sauce, add additional cream or olive oil and process until combined.
10. Drain vermicelli in colander and divide among 4 dinner plates. Spoon sauce over vermicelli and garnish with lime wedges and diced bell pepper.

Tropical Salad

½ pound jícama or Jerusalem artichokes
Large mango or small cantaloupe (about 1 pound)
Large pink grapefruit
Large avocado
Small bunch each watercress and coriander
6 tablespoons good-quality olive oil
Salt and freshly ground pepper

1. Peel jícama or Jerusalem artichokes, cut into 1½ by ¼-inch strips, and place in medium-size nonaluminum bowl. Peel mango, cut into ½-inch cubes, and add to bowl. Peel grapefruit, removing white pith. Section grapefruit over small bowl to catch juice; reserve 2 tablespoons juice. Add grapefruit sections to medium-size bowl.
2. Peel avocado, halve lengthwise, and discard pit. Cut avocado into ½-inch cubes, add to bowl, and toss.
3. Wash, dry, and trim watercress and coriander. Add watercress to bowl. Finely chop enough coriander to measure 2 tablespoons.
4. In small jar with tight-fitting lid, combine oil, 2 tablespoons grapefruit juice, chopped coriander, and salt and pepper to taste and shake to blend; set aside until needed.
5. Just before serving, shake dressing to recombine. Pour dressing over salad and toss. Divide salad among 4 plates.

Mexican Hot Chocolate

1½ ounces Mexican chocolate
1 quart milk
¼ cup unsweetened cocoa powder
6 tablespoons sugar
Pinch each of salt and freshly grated nutmeg
2 to 3 tablespoons Kahlúa
1 teaspoon vanilla extract
4 cinnamon sticks

1. Coarsely chop chocolate. Heat chocolate, milk, cocoa, sugar, salt, and nutmeg in medium-size heavy-gauge saucepan over medium heat, stirring frequently, 3 to 4 minutes, or just until mixture comes to a boil. Remove from heat.
2. Stir in Kahlúa and vanilla and divide among 4 mugs. Garnish with cinnamon sticks.

Deborah Madison

MENU 1 (Right)
Pan Bagna with Green Sauce
Eggplant Salad with Basil and Lemon
Dried Figs with Chèvre and Almonds

MENU 2
Fennel and Watercress Soup
Artichoke Salad

MENU 3
Curried Lentil Soup with Ginger
Raita
Wilted Spinach Salad

Dairy products, legumes, and fresh vegetables of all types play an important role in Deborah Madison's cooking. Although she is not a strict vegetarian, she likes to create new and intriguing recipes that utilize these ingredients.

She describes Menu 1 as "a picnic at the table" to be served indoors or out. It features her version of *pan bagna*—a sort of *salade Niçoise* on a roll—popular in the south of France. Here the roll is hollowed out and filled with a vegetable, cheese, and avocado salad dressed with a piquant green sauce. A second warm, lemony salad of eggplant is presented with the sandwich, and, for dessert, Deborah Madison offers the simple but sophisticated combination of dried figs, chèvre, and almonds.

Perfect for cool weather dining, Menu 2 pairs a creamy fennel soup with a salad of artichokes, mushrooms, and fontina. The salad should be served at room temperature so the cheese will be most flavorful. The two dishes are tasty together but, if you prefer, the soup can precede the salad or vice versa.

Menu 3 is an Indian-inspired meal of curried lentil soup and refreshing chilled *raita*, or yogurt "salad." The cook flavors the yogurt with scallions and fresh mint and adds raisins and pistachios as well. The accompanying spinach salad is tossed with olive oil, garlic, and a small dried red chili if desired.

Just right for a casual meal: hollowed-out rolls filled with a mélange of vegetables and cheese and served with eggplant salad. Dried figs and almonds go well with chèvre for dessert.

44

Pan Bagna with Green Sauce
Eggplant Salad with Basil and Lemon
Dried Figs with Chèvre and Almonds

When preparing the *pan bagna* for this delightful picnic-style meal, select medium or small rolls. Although large rolls might make attractive containers for the salad, they are difficult to manage when eating. You can use pita breads instead of rolls, but if you do, fill them just before serving rather than preparing them in advance, or the moist filling will make the bread soggy. If you wish, line each pita with several lettuce leaves.

The accompanying green sauce calls for Kalamata olives, dark purple vinegar-cured Greek olives. Their slightly firm but juicy flesh makes them a popular eating olive in all Mediterranean countries. Look for these olives in Greek or Middle Eastern markets or specialty food shops, and refrigerate them in a tightly closed container.

The cook suggests using Japanese eggplants for the salad. Smaller than other varieties, this type of eggplant is so sweet and tender it can be cooked without preliminary salting to remove bitter juices. Look for Japanese eggplants in Oriental markets and well-stocked supermarkets. If necessary, substitute any small eggplants available.

WHAT TO DRINK

A young, simple wine, either white or red (but in either case slightly chilled), makes a natural partner for this meal. Try a dry French Vouvray, a dry California Chenin Blanc, or an Italian Soave for a white; a French Beaujolais, a California Zinfandel, or an Italian Chianti for a red.

SHOPPING LIST AND STAPLES

1½ pounds Japanese eggplants (3 or 4)
4 firm, ripe tomatoes (about 1¼ pounds total weight)
Large red bell pepper
Medium-size cucumber
Small red onion
Medium-size clove garlic, plus 1 clove (optional)
Small bunch fresh parsley, or large bunch if using dried basil
Several small bunches fresh herbs, such as thyme, hyssop, mint, marjoram, and/or summer savory, or 1 teaspoon mixed dried herbs
Small bunch fresh basil, or 1 teaspoon dried
Medium-size avocado
Medium-size lemon
½ pound chèvre

6 to 8 ounces feta cheese
11-ounce jar Kalamata olives
2-ounce jar capers
¾ cup good-quality olive oil
2 tablespoons champagne vinegar or red wine vinegar
½ cup walnuts
¾ cup whole shelled almonds
4 medium-size round hard rolls
4½-ounce package water biscuits or other unsalted crackers
12-ounce package dried black mission figs
12-ounce package dried Calimyrna figs
4-ounce jar sun-dried tomatoes (optional)
Salt and freshly ground pepper

UTENSILS

Large skillet with cover
2 large bowls
Small nonaluminum bowl
Strainer
Measuring cups and spoons
Chef's knife
Paring knife
Wooden spoon
Grater
Vegetable peeler (optional)

START-TO-FINISH STEPS

1. Peel garlic and mince 1 clove for salad recipe and 1 clove, if using, for green sauce recipe. Wash and dry parsley, and other fresh herbs, if using. If using basil, set aside 16 to 20 large leaves for pan bagna recipe and finely chop enough remaining basil to measure ½ cup for salad recipe. If not using fresh basil, finely chop enough parsley to measure 2 to 3 tablespoons for salad recipe. Finely chop enough remaining parsley to measure ½ cup for green sauce recipe. Finely chop enough other fresh herbs, if using, to measure 2 tablespoons total for green sauce recipe.
2. Follow green sauce recipe steps 1 and 2.
3. Follow pan bagna recipe steps 1 through 5.
4. Follow salad recipe steps 1 through 3.
5. While eggplant is cooking, follow figs recipe step 1.
6. Follow pan bagna recipe step 6, salad recipe steps 4 and 5, and serve.
7. Serve figs for dessert.

Pan Bagna with Green Sauce

Large red bell pepper
4 firm, ripe tomatoes (about 1¼ pounds
   total weight)
Medium-size avocado
Small red onion
Medium-size cucumber
6 to 8 ounces feta cheese
Green Sauce (see following recipe)
Freshly ground pepper
4 medium-size round hard rolls
16 to 20 large basil leaves (optional)

1. Wash bell pepper and tomatoes and dry with paper towels. Halve, core, and seed pepper and cut into thin strips. Halve, core, seed, and coarsely chop tomatoes.
2. Halve, pit, and peel avocado and cut into ½-inch chunks. Peel, halve, and thinly slice onion. Peel and slice or coarsely chop cucumber.
3. Crumble feta into large bowl.
4. Add vegetables to feta. Add green sauce and toss gently until thoroughly combined. Season salad with ground pepper to taste.
5. Using bread knife, cut off top third of each roll; set aside. Pull out soft bread from inside of rolls; reserve for another use, if desired. Fill hollowed-out rolls with salad and replace tops. Set aside sandwiches and any remaining salad at room temperature until ready to serve.
6. To serve, divide sandwiches among 4 dinner plates. Arrange 4 or 5 basil leaves, if using, on each plate and top with remaining salad.

Green Sauce

1 tablespoon capers
5 Kalamata olives
½ cup walnuts
½ cup finely chopped fresh parsley
2 tablespoons finely chopped fresh herbs, such as thyme,
   hyssop, mint, marjoram, and/or summer savory, or
   1 teaspoon mixed dried herbs
Medium-size clove garlic, minced (optional)
½ cup good-quality olive oil
2 tablespoons champagne vinegar or
   red wine vinegar

1. Drain capers in strainer and chop finely. Drain and pit olives and chop coarsely. Finely chop walnuts.
2. Combine capers, olives, walnuts, parsley and other herbs, garlic if using, oil, and vinegar in small non-aluminum bowl and stir until well blended. Set aside until needed, and reblend if necessary.

Eggplant Salad with Basil and Lemon

Medium-size lemon
1½ pounds Japanese eggplants (3 or 4)
Medium-size sun-dried tomato (optional)
¼ cup good-quality olive oil
½ cup finely chopped fresh basil, or 2 to 3 tablespoons
   finely chopped fresh parsley and 1 teaspoon dried basil
Medium-size clove garlic, minced
Salt and freshly ground pepper

1. Wash lemon and dry with paper towel. Grate enough lemon rind to measure 1 tablespoon. Reserve lemon for another use.
2. Peel eggplants and cut enough into ¼-inch cubes to measure about 6 cups. Thinly slice sun-dried tomato, if using.
3. Heat oil in large skillet over medium-high heat until hot. Add eggplant cubes and stir to coat with oil. Continue to cook over medium-high heat, stirring frequently, 5 minutes. Add ¼ cup water, cover pan, and reduce heat to medium. Cook, stirring occasionally, 10 to 15 minutes, or until eggplant is tender. (Add additional water to prevent sticking, if necessary.)
4. Combine eggplant, lemon rind, tomato, herbs, and garlic in large bowl. Add salt and pepper to taste and stir well.
5. Divide salad among 4 dinner plates.

Dried Figs with Chèvre and Almonds

6 to 8 dried black mission figs
6 to 8 dried Calimyrna figs
¾ cup whole shelled almonds
½ pound chèvre
4½-ounce package water biscuits or other unsalted
   crackers

1. Arrange figs, almonds, chèvre, and biscuits decoratively on cutting board or serving platter. Set aside at room temperature until ready to serve.

Fennel and Watercress Soup
Artichoke Salad

A vegetable and cheese salad with a tangy vinaigrette provides a flavor counterpoint to fennel and watercress soup.

The vegetable and cheese salad features artichokes, which are abundant year round. If you can find tender baby artichokes, select them instead of medium-size artichokes; they have no interior choke and the stems are so tender they can also be eaten. You can use canned artichoke hearts but be sure to rinse and drain them very well before using them.

Smooth, mellow fontina is a semi-soft Italian cheese available in cheese shops and well-stocked supermarkets. If it is unavailable, use Gruyère or Emmenthaler instead.

WHAT TO DRINK

The cook suggests a dry Italian white wine to accompany this meal. Choose Trebbiano, Frascati, or Pino Bianco.

SHOPPING LIST AND STAPLES

1½ pounds fennel
4 medium-size artichokes (about 1½ pounds total weight)
4 to 6 ounces fresh mushrooms
Small bunch celery
Large head Belgian endive
Small head chicory
Small bunch watercress
Medium-size yellow onion
2 shallots
Small clove garlic
2 large lemons
2 cups milk, approximately
3 tablespoons unsalted butter
6 to 8 ounces fontina cheese
5 cups vegetable or chicken stock, preferably homemade, see page 9 (optional)
7-ounce jar pimiento-stuffed green olives
½ cup plus 1 tablespoon good-quality olive oil
3 tablespoons tarragon vinegar
1 teaspoon Dijon mustard
Salt
Freshly ground pepper

UTENSILS

Food processor (optional)
Blender
Large stockpot with cover
Large nonaluminum skillet with cover
2 large bowls, 1 nonaluminum
Small bowl
Colander
Fine strainer
Measuring cups and spoons
Chef's knife
Paring knife
Wooden spoon
Citrus juicer (optional)
Whisk
Ladle

START-TO-FINISH STEPS

1. Follow soup recipe steps 1 through 3 and salad recipe steps 1 through 3.
2. Follow soup recipe step 4.
3. While soup is cooking, follow salad recipe steps 4 through 8.
4. Follow soup recipe step 5 and salad recipe steps 9 through 12.
5. Follow soup recipe steps 6 through 8 and salad recipe step 13.
6. Follow soup recipe step 9 and serve with salad.

RECIPES

Fennel and Watercress Soup

3 tablespoons unsalted butter
Small bunch watercress
1½ pounds fennel
Medium-size yellow onion
1 teaspoon salt, approximately
5 cups vegetable or chicken stock, or water
2 cups milk, approximately

1. Melt 2 tablespoons butter with ½ cup water in large stockpot over medium-low heat.
2. Meanwhile, wash watercress and fennel and dry with paper towels. Trim and discard tough stems from watercress and set sprigs aside. Trim fennel bulb and slice thinly. Peel, halve, and thinly slice onion.
3. Add fennel, onion, and 1 teaspoon salt to stockpot and cook, covered, over medium-low heat 10 minutes.
4. Add stock or water, increase heat to medium-high, and bring mixture to a boil. Reduce heat to medium and cook soup, partially covered, 15 minutes, or until vegetables are soft.
5. Remove pot from heat and set soup aside to cool 10 minutes.
6. When cool, turn soup into food processor or blender and process 1 minute. (Process in batches if necessary.) Force soup through fine strainer into stockpot, pressing gently to extract as much liquid as possible. Discard any solids remaining in strainer.
7. Add enough milk to thin soup to desired consistency. Add additional salt to taste and reheat soup over low heat.
8. Meanwhile, place watercress in food processor or blender and process until coarsely puréed, adding a little water if necessary.
9. When soup is hot, stir remaining 1 tablespoon butter into soup. Stir in watercress and ladle soup into 4 bowls.

Artichoke Salad

2 large lemons
4 medium-size artichokes (about 1½ pounds total weight)
1½ teaspoons salt, approximately
2 large stalks celery
Small head chicory

49

Large head Belgian endive
2 shallots
Small clove garlic
4 to 6 ounces fresh mushrooms
6 to 8 ounces fontina cheese
16 to 20 pimiento-stuffed green olives
½ cup plus 1 tablespoon good-quality olive oil
3 tablespoons tarragon vinegar
1 teaspoon Dijon mustard
Freshly ground pepper

1. Halve lemons and squeeze enough juice to measure 5 tablespoons.
2. Combine 2 cups water and 1½ tablespoons lemon juice in large nonaluminum bowl.
3. Wash artichokes and dry with paper towels. Trim and peel stems and discard tough outer leaves. Cut off top inch of leaves from each artichoke (see illustration below) and quarter artichokes lengthwise. Using sharp paring knife, remove chokes and discard. Cut artichokes lengthwise into ½-inch-thick wedges. Place in bowl of lemon water.

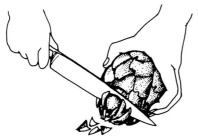

Trim top inch of leaves from artichokes.

4. Bring 1 inch water, 1½ tablespoons lemon juice, and 1 teaspoon salt to a boil in large nonaluminum skillet over high heat.
5. Place artichokes in skillet of boiling water, reduce heat to medium, and simmer, covered, 5 minutes, or until artichokes are firm-tender. Discard lemon water.
6. Meanwhile, wash celery, chicory, and endive, and dry with paper towels. Thinly slice celery. Tear chicory into bite-size pieces. Trim endive, halve lengthwise, and slice diagonally. Place chicory and endive in large bowl and set aside. Peel and mince shallots and garlic.
7. Turn artichokes into colander, refresh under cold running water, and allow to drain.
8. Meanwhile, wipe mushrooms clean with damp paper towels and slice thinly. Cut fontina into bite-size pieces. Drain olives in strainer; set aside.

9. Combine celery, mushrooms, fontina, and 1 tablespoon olive oil in large bowl. Add remaining 2 tablespoons lemon juice and toss to coat well.
10. For vinaigrette, combine shallots, garlic, vinegar, mustard, and ½ teaspoon salt in small bowl. Whisk in remaining ½ cup olive oil and continue to whisk until well blended.
11. Add artichokes and olives to vegetables and cheese. Pour in half of vinaigrette and toss gently. Season with salt and pepper to taste and toss again.
12. Add remaining vinaigrette to chicory and endive and toss well.
13. Divide greens among 4 dinner plates and top with artichoke mixture.

ADDED TOUCH

For this dessert, pears are filled with a mixture of Italian *amaretti* (crisp almond-flavored cookies) and almonds. If you like, softly whip the heavy cream and flavor it with *amaretto*, the Italian almond-flavored liqueur.

Baked Pears with Almond Filling

2 large firm pears such as Anjou, Bosc, or Comice (about 1 pound total weight)
6 amaretti
¼ cup shelled almonds (2 ounces)
1 tablespoon sugar
3 tablespoons unsalted butter
1 cup heavy cream (optional)

1. Preheat oven to 400 degrees.
2. Peel and halve pears. Using melon baller or teaspoon, remove cores and make a hollow in each half. Cut thin slice from rounded side of each half to keep pears from tipping over in baking dish.
3. Place amaretti on sheet of waxed paper and crush with rolling pin into coarse crumbs. Chop almonds very finely.
4. Combine amaretti, almonds, sugar, and 2 tablespoons butter in small bowl. Work with fingers to form a paste.
5. Divide paste among hollows in pear halves and place pears in 8-inch square baking dish with ¼ cup water. Dot pear halves with remaining 1 tablespoon butter. Cover pan with foil and bake pears 25 to 35 minutes, or until tender. (Time will depend on size and type of pear.)
6. Divide pears among 4 dessert dishes and serve with cream, if desired.

Curried Lentil Soup with Ginger
Raita
Wilted Spinach Salad

For a taste of India, offer curried lentil soup, raita *garnished with mint, and warm spinach salad.*

The lentil soup owes its intense flavor to fresh ginger and freshly ground spices. An indispensable ingredient in all Oriental cuisines, fresh ginger is sold at most well-stocked supermarkets and at greengrocers. Select a firm, pale brown root with unwrinkled skin. To store ginger, wrap it in a paper towel, then a plastic bag, and refrigerate it for up to a month. Check weekly for mold, however. Or, if you prefer, store it in the freezer, where it will last about three months. The cook recommends adjusting the proportion of spices to suit your own taste. If whole spices are unavailable, you can use commercially ground spices, but be sure they are fresh.

The spinach salad, which is equally good served warm or at room temperature, can be made with other greens, such as beet tops or Swiss chard. These greens require longer cooking, but otherwise the method is the same. Drain the greens well to prevent excess water from diluting the garlicky oil dressing.

WHAT TO DRINK

Iced mint tea, cold beer, or a well-chilled spicy white wine such as Gewürztraminer would go well with these zesty dishes.

51

2 pounds spinach
Small bunch celery
Medium-size carrot
Small bunch scallions
Medium-size onion
2 medium-size cloves garlic
1-inch piece fresh ginger
Small bunch fresh coriander
Small bunch fresh mint or basil, or small bunch fresh parsley and 1 teaspoon dried mint or basil
Small lemon
4 tablespoons unsalted butter
1 pint low-fat plain yogurt
7 cups vegetable or chicken stock, preferably homemade, see page 9 (optional)
¼ cup good-quality olive oil
1½ cups brown lentils
3 tablespoons unsalted shelled pistachio nuts or walnuts
2 tablespoons golden raisins
Small dried red chili (optional)
Bay leaf
1 teaspoon each mustard, cumin, and coriander seeds
1 teaspoon ground turmeric
1½-inch cinnamon stick, or ½ teaspoon ground cinnamon
3 whole cloves, or ¼ teaspoon ground cloves
¼ teaspoon Cayenne pepper, approximately
Salt

UTENSILS

Blender
Large stockpot
Large skillet
3-quart saucepan with cover
2 large bowls
2 small bowls
Colander
Strainer
Measuring cups and spoons
Chef's knife
Paring knife
Wooden spoon
Ladle
Electric coffee mill or spice grinder (optional)

START-TO-FINISH STEPS

1. Peel garlic for soup and salad recipes. Thinly slice 1 clove for salad recipe.
2. Follow salad recipe steps 1 and 2.
3. Follow soup recipe steps 1 through 4.
4. While lentils cook, follow raita recipe steps 1 and 2.
5. Follow salad recipe steps 3 through 5.
6. Follow soup recipe steps 5 through 7.
7. While soup cooks, follow raita recipe steps 3 through 5.
8. Follow salad recipe step 6, soup recipe steps 8 and 9, and serve with raita and salad.

RECIPES

Curried Lentil Soup with Ginger

Medium-size carrot
2 stalks celery
Small bunch fresh coriander
Medium-size onion
1 teaspoon mustard seeds
1 teaspoon cumin seeds
1 teaspoon coriander seeds
1½-inch cinnamon stick, or ½ teaspoon ground cinnamon
3 whole cloves, or ¼ teaspoon ground cloves
1 teaspoon ground turmeric
¼ teaspoon Cayenne pepper
1-inch piece fresh ginger
Medium-size clove garlic, peeled
1½ cups brown lentils
7 cups vegetable or chicken stock, or water
Salt
Bay leaf
4 tablespoons unsalted butter

1. Wash and dry carrot, celery, and fresh coriander. Trim and peel carrot. Coarsely chop carrot and celery. Coarsely chop enough coriander leaves to measure 1 tablespoon; set aside. Peel onion and cut into small dice.
2. Place mustard, cumin, and coriander seeds, and cinnamon stick and whole cloves if using, in electric coffee mill, spice grinder, or blender, and grind to a powder. Combine with remaining spices in small bowl. If using blender, do not rinse container.
3. Peel and halve fresh ginger and place in blender with garlic and ½ cup water. Process until puréed. Set mixture aside in blender.

4. Pick over lentils and remove any bits of debris. Rinse lentils in strainer and turn into 3-quart saucepan with stock or water, salt to taste, and bay leaf. Bring to a boil over medium-high heat, reduce heat to medium, and cook at a slow boil, covered, 15 minutes, or until lentils are soft.
5. Melt butter in large skillet over medium heat. Add carrot, celery, and onion, and cook over low heat 5 to 6 minutes, or until vegetables are softened.
6. Add spice mixture and ginger-garlic purée to vegetables and stir to combine. Cook 1 minute.
7. When lentils are soft, add vegetable mixture to saucepan, reduce heat to low, and cook another 5 minutes. Remove and discard bay leaf.
8. Place 1 cup soup in blender and process until puréed. Return purée to soup and add salt to taste. (If desired, thin soup with additional stock or water.)
9. Ladle soup into 4 soup bowls and sprinkle with chopped coriander.

Raita

2 tablespoons golden raisins
2 large scallions
Small bunch fresh mint or basil, or small bunch fresh parsley and 1 teaspoon dried mint or basil
3 tablespoons unsalted shelled pistachio nuts or walnuts
2 cups low-fat plain yogurt
⅛ teaspoon salt
Pinch of Cayenne pepper (optional)

1. Place raisins in small bowl with warm water to cover and allow to soak 15 minutes.
2. Meanwhile, wash scallions and fresh mint, basil, or parsley, and dry with paper towels. Mince scallions. Set aside several sprigs of herbs for garnish, and mince enough leaves to measure 2 tablespoons. Finely chop nuts.
3. Drain raisins in strainer and press out excess water.
4. Combine raisins, scallions, mint, basil and/or parsley, nuts, yogurt, and salt in large bowl and toss well.
5. Divide raita among 4 small bowls. Garnish with herbs and dust with Cayenne, if desired.

Wilted Spinach Salad

3 tablespoons salt
2 pounds spinach
Small lemon
Small dried red chili (optional)

Medium-size clove garlic, thinly sliced
¼ cup good-quality olive oil

1. Bring 6 quarts water and salt to a boil in large stockpot over high heat.
2. Meanwhile, wash spinach in several changes of tepid water. Do not dry. Trim tough ends from spinach. Wash lemon; cut into 4 wedges and set aside. Seed and dice chili, if using.
3. Plunge spinach into boiling water and cook 1 to 2 minutes, or just until leaves turn bright green. Turn spinach into colander to drain.
4. Meanwhile, combine chili, if using, garlic, and olive oil in large bowl.
5. Squeeze spinach to remove as much water as possible and chop coarsely. Add to bowl and toss gently. Set aside until ready to serve.
6. To serve, divide spinach among 4 dinner plates and garnish with lemon wedges.

<hr>

ADDED TOUCH

A sparkling tangerine ice makes a simple and refreshing conclusion to any meal. The exact number of tangerines needed will depend on their juiciness.

Tangerine Ice

3 pounds tangerines
Small lemon
¾ cup sugar
Small bunch mint for garnish (optional)

1. Wash and dry 2 tangerines; grate enough rind to measure 2 tablespoons and place in medium-size bowl.
2. Halve tangerines and squeeze enough juice to measure 3 cups; add to bowl. Halve and juice lemon; set aside.
3. Place sugar and 2 tablespoons tangerine juice in small saucepan. Cook over medium heat, stirring, until sugar is dissolved. Remove from heat and cool until syrup is tepid.
4. When cooled, add sugar syrup to remaining tangerine juice and rind. Add lemon juice, a drop at a time, to taste.
5. Turn mixture into container of ice cream freezer and freeze according to manufacturer's directions until the ice is soft and creamy. (If necessary, let ice soften in the refrigerator before serving.)
6. Just before serving, wash and dry mint, if using, and separate into sprigs. Scoop ice into dessert dishes and garnish with mint sprigs, if desired.

Jeanne Jones

MENU 1 (Left)
Gazpacho
Tamale Pie
Guacamole Salad

MENU 2
Parsley Salad with Tarragon Vinaigrette
Cheddar Soufflé
Herbed Vegetables

MENU 3
Arugula and Radicchio Salad with
Warm Mushroom Dressing
Pasta Florentine
Braised Tomatoes

As an author, lecturer, and consultant in the nutrition field, Jeanne Jones believes that people who love to cook and eat can remain slender without feeling deprived. For a well-balanced daily diet, she reduces or eliminates obvious sources of fat and increases the number of high-fiber plant foods that, she says, "satisfy one's physiological and psychological desire for food." All three of her menus adhere to these principles, yet none of the dishes tastes "dietetic" or looks skimpy and unappetizing.

Menu 1 proves that Mexican-style food, generally considered fattening fare, need not be forbidden to waistline watchers. The gazpacho is a delicate blend of chopped raw vegetables combined with tomato juice, cumin, and Worcestershire sauce. The tamale pie is well-seasoned mixture of vegetables, cheese, and cornmeal. For a change of pace, you can serve the soup or the accompanying guacamole salad as a first course.

Perfect for lunch or dinner, Menu 2 features a cheese soufflé prepared with low-fat rather than whole milk. Jeanne Jones also offers two compatible vegetable dishes: an unusual parsley, Parmesan cheese, and tomato salad tossed with an herb vinaigrette as an appetizer, and lightly steamed and sautéed carrots, zucchini, and cauliflower sprinkled with thyme.

By using low-fat milk and two low-fat cheeses in the pasta Florentine of Menu 3, the cook transforms a Northern Italian dish that is generally heavy into a lighter main course. Braised tomatoes flavored with basil and an arugula and radicchio salad with an unusual warm mushroom dressing go well with the pasta.

Chunky gazpacho, cheese-topped tamale pie, and guacamole salad with tortilla chips are the makings of a complete Mexican meal. Perfect for informal dining—indoors or out—these dishes can easily be served buffet style.

55

Gazpacho
Tamale Pie
Guacamole Salad

Gazpacho is a refreshing soup that tastes best when made with vegetables at their flavor peak. A typical gazpacho calls for puréed onions, tomatoes, green peppers, garlic, and cucumbers. For this version, the cook chops the vegetables coarsely to give the soup a crunchier texture.

For maximum flavor in the guacamole salad, use perfectly ripe avocados. A ripe avocado is slightly soft to the touch. You can ripen an avocado by wrapping it in a brown paper bag and leaving it at room temperature for a few days. To test for ripeness, stick a toothpick into the stem end. If the toothpick moves in and out easily, the avocado is ripe. Refrigerate ripe avocados for up to five days.

WHAT TO DRINK

Select a Mexican beer or a robust ale here. If you prefer wine, choose a simple white, such as an Italian Soave.

SHOPPING LIST AND STAPLES

Small head iceberg lettuce
2 medium-size tomatoes (about 1 pound total weight)
Small cucumber
Small green bell pepper
Small bunch scallions
2 large onions
1 large and 2 small cloves garlic
Small bunch coriander (optional)
2 medium-size ripe avocados
2 lemons
1 egg
1½ cups buttermilk
1 tablespoon margarine
6 ounces sharp Cheddar cheese
16-ounce can crushed tomatoes
7-ounce can chopped green chilies
7-ounce can corn kernels
18-ounce can tomato juice
½ teaspoon Worcestershire sauce
¼ teaspoon hot pepper sauce
½ cup yellow cornmeal
7½-ounce bag tortilla chips
1 tablespoon chili powder
1 teaspoon dried oregano
½ teaspoon dried basil
⅜ teaspoon ground cumin

¼ teaspoon dried thyme
Salt
Freshly ground black pepper

UTENSILS

Food processor (optional)
Large skillet
Small saucepan
Shallow 2-quart baking dish or four individual gratin dishes
Large nonaluminum bowl
Small bowl
Strainer
Measuring cups and spoons
Chef's knife
Wooden spoon
Grater (if not using food processor)
Citrus juicer (optional)
Whisk
Mortar and pestle (optional)

START-TO-FINISH STEPS

1. Wash tomatoes, lemons, and scallions, and dry with paper towels. Halve, core, and dice 1 tomato each for gazpacho and guacamole recipes. Cut thin slice from 1 lemon, cut slice in half, and reserve for garnish for gazpacho recipe. Squeeze enough lemon juice to measure 2 tablespoons for gazpacho recipe and 1 tablespoon for guacamole recipe. Trim scallions. Thinly slice enough scallions crosswise to measure 3 tablespoons for gazpacho recipe and finely chop enough to measure 1 tablespoon for guacamole recipe. Peel garlic; mince 1 small clove each for gazpacho and guacamole recipes and mince large clove for tamale pie recipe. Peel onions. Coarsely chop 1 onion each for gazpacho and tamale pie recipes. Drain chilies in strainer for guacamole and tamale pie recipes.
2. Follow gazpacho recipe steps 1 and 2.
3. Follow tamale pie recipe steps 1 through 7.
4. While pie is baking, follow guacamole recipe steps 1 through 3.
5. Follow tamale pie recipe step 8.
6. While pie continues to bake, follow gazpacho recipe step 3 and guacamole recipe step 4.
7. Follow tamale pie recipe step 9 and serve with gazpacho and guacamole.

RECIPES

Gazpacho

Small cucumber
Small green bell pepper
Large onion, coarsely chopped
Small clove garlic, minced
Medium-size tomato, diced
2 cups tomato juice
⅛ teaspoon ground cumin
½ teaspoon Worcestershire sauce
¼ teaspoon freshly ground black pepper
2 tablespoons lemon juice
3 tablespoons thinly sliced scallions
1 slice lemon, halved

1. Peel, halve, seed, and coarsely chop cucumber. Wash bell pepper and dry with paper towel. Halve, core, seed, and coarsely chop pepper.
2. In large serving bowl, combine cucumber, bell pepper, onion, garlic, tomato, tomato juice, cumin, Worcestershire sauce, ground pepper, and lemon juice. Cover bowl and place in refrigerator to chill at least 30 minutes.
3. Just before serving, remove gazpacho from refrigerator and garnish with scallions and lemon slice.

Tamale Pie

7-ounce can corn kernels
6 ounces sharp Cheddar cheese
¼ teaspoon dried thyme
½ teaspoon dried basil
1 teaspoon dried oregano
1 tablespoon margarine
Large onion, coarsely chopped
Large clove garlic, minced
¾ cup canned chopped green chilies, drained
16-ounce can crushed tomatoes
1 tablespoon chili powder
¼ teaspoon ground cumin
¼ teaspoon salt
1½ cups buttermilk
½ cup yellow cornmeal
1 egg

1. Preheat oven to 350 degrees.
2. Drain corn in strainer. Using food processor or grater, grate enough cheese to measure 1½ cups. Crush thyme, basil, and oregano in mortar with pestle, or crush herbs between fingers.
3. Melt margarine in large skillet over medium-high heat. Add onion and garlic and sauté over medium heat 2 to 3 minutes, or until soft.
4. Add corn, crushed herbs, chilies, tomatoes and their juice, chili powder, cumin, and salt to skillet. Stir to combine and cook 8 to 10 minutes.
5. Meanwhile, combine buttermilk and cornmeal in small saucepan and bring to a boil over medium heat. Reduce heat and cook, whisking constantly, 3 to 4 minutes, or until mixture is thickened. Remove pan from heat, add egg, and stir well to blend.
6. Add cornmeal mixture to skillet and stir until all ingredients are well combined. Turn mixture into shallow 2-quart baking dish or four individual gratin dishes.
7. Place pie in oven and bake, uncovered, 20 minutes.
8. Sprinkle top of pie with grated cheese and bake another 5 to 10 minutes, or until cheese is melted.
9. Remove pie from oven and serve immediately.

Guacamole Salad

Small head iceberg lettuce
Small bunch coriander (optional)
2 medium-size ripe avocados
1 tablespoon finely chopped scallion
Small clove garlic, minced
1 tablespoon lemon juice
2 tablespoons canned chopped green chilies, drained
¼ teaspoon hot pepper sauce
Medium-size tomato, diced
¼ teaspoon salt
7½-ounce bag tortilla chips

1. Wash and dry lettuce, and coriander if using. Reserve 4 large lettuce leaves; shred remaining lettuce. Place in plastic bag and refrigerate. Reserve 1 sprig coriander for garnish; mince enough remaining coriander to measure 1 tablespoon.
2. Halve avocados lengthwise and discard pits. Scoop out flesh into small bowl and mash with fork.
3. In large nonaluminum bowl, combine minced coriander, if using, scallion, garlic, lemon juice, chilies, hot pepper sauce, tomato, and salt. Add avocado and mix well. Cover bowl and place in refrigerator until ready to serve.
4. To serve, line platter with lettuce leaves and top with shredded lettuce. Mound guacamole in center, garnish with coriander sprig, and surround with tortilla chips.

Parsley Salad with Tarragon Vinaigrette
Cheddar Soufflé
Herbed Vegetables

For this elegant dinner, serve the parsley salad, then bring out the herbed vegetables and—finally—the soufflé.

A soufflé is a light, puffy creation that is impressive at any meal. Although the idea of preparing a soufflé intimidates many cooks, mastering the technique is simple if you follow these pointers. Use a nonaluminum bowl for beating the whites and be sure the bowl and beaters are grease free. Allow the eggs to come to room temperature before beating: Cold egg whites will not achieve as great a volume. Beat the egg whites until they stand in stiff but not dry peaks. When folding the whites into the soufflé base, do not overmix or the whites will deflate; a few streaks of egg white are acceptable.

Prepare the soufflé dish as follows: Butter the dish, then dust it with flour. If you think that the soufflé batter will fill the dish to within 1 inch of the rim, add a foil "collar." Make a 4-inch-wide strip of doubled foil to fit around the dish and overlap 1 inch. Butter and flour one side of the strip, then tie it, floured-side in, around the dish with string. The collar should extend 2 inches above the rim of the soufflé dish.

WHAT TO DRINK

The cook suggests a white wine such as a California Chardonnay or Pinot Blanc with this menu.

Small head cauliflower
2 medium-size zucchini (about 1 pound total weight)
2 large carrots (about ½ pound total weight)
Large clove garlic
Small bunch fresh thyme, or 1 teaspoon dried
Large bunch curly parsley
Small lemon
5 large eggs
1 cup low-fat milk
4 tablespoons unsalted butter or margarine
2 ounces Parmesan cheese, preferably imported
3 ounces sharp Cheddar cheese
2 tablespoons good-quality olive oil, preferably
　　extra-virgin
2 tablespoons tarragon vinegar
1 teaspoon Worcestershire sauce
6½-ounce jar sun-dried tomatoes, or 1 pint cherry
　　tomatoes
½ teaspoon Dijon mustard
3 tablespoons all-purpose flour
1 teaspoon sugar
¼ teaspoon dried tarragon
¼ teaspoon dried basil
⅛ teaspoon cream of tartar
Cayenne pepper
Salt and freshly ground pepper

UTENSILS

Food processor (optional)
Electric mixer
Large skillet
Large saucepan with cover
Medium-size saucepan
Collapsible vegetable steamer
2-quart soufflé dish
Large nonaluminum or glass bowl
Small bowl
Salad spinner (optional)
Colander
Measuring cups and spoons
Chef's knife
Paring knife
Grater (if not using food processor)
2 wooden spoons
Rubber spatula
Citrus juicer (optional)
Whisk
Mortar and pestle (optional)

START-TO-FINISH STEPS

One hour ahead: Set out eggs to come to room temperature for soufflé recipe.

1. Using food processor or grater, grate enough Parmesan to measure ½ cup for salad recipe and enough Cheddar to

measure ¾ cup for soufflé recipe.
2. Follow vinaigrette recipe steps 1 through 4.
3. Follow vegetables recipe steps 1 through 4.
4. Follow salad recipe steps 1 and 2.
5. Follow soufflé recipe steps 1 through 8.
6. While soufflé is baking, follow salad recipe step 3 and serve as first course.
7. Five minutes before soufflé is done, follow vegetables recipe step 5.
8. Follow soufflé recipe step 9 and serve with vegetables.

RECIPES

Parsley Salad with Tarragon Vinaigrette

Large bunch curly parsley
½ cup sun-dried tomatoes, or 8 cherry tomatoes
Tarragon Vinaigrette (see following recipe)
½ cup grated Parmesan cheese

1. Wash parsley and dry in salad spinner or with paper towels. Trim parsley. Remove enough small sprigs from stems to measure about 4 cups. Place parsley sprigs in large salad bowl, cover, and refrigerate until needed. Cut sun-dried tomatoes lengthwise into thin slices. Or, wash and dry cherry tomatoes, if using. Remove and discard stems and quarter tomatoes.
2. Add tomatoes to tarragon vinaigrette and return vinaigrette to refrigerator until needed.
3. Just before serving, remove parsley from refrigerator and sprinkle with Parmesan cheese. Add dressing and toss.

Tarragon Vinaigrette

Small lemon
Large clove garlic
¼ teaspoon dried tarragon
¼ teaspoon dried basil
2 tablespoons tarragon vinegar
2 tablespoons good-quality olive oil, preferably
　　extra-virgin
½ teaspoon Dijon mustard
½ teaspoon Worcestershire sauce
1 teaspoon sugar
⅛ teaspoon salt
Freshly ground pepper

1. Halve lemon and squeeze enough juice from one half to measure 2 teaspoons; reserve remaining half for another use. Peel and mince garlic clove. Crush tarragon and basil in mortar with pestle, or crush herbs with fingers. Set aside.
2. Combine vinegar, olive oil, ¼ cup water, mustard, and Worcestershire sauce in small nonaluminum bowl and whisk until well combined.
3. Add lemon juice, garlic, crushed herbs, sugar, salt, and pepper to taste and whisk again.
4. Cover bowl with plastic wrap and place dressing in refrigerator until needed.

Cheddar Soufflé

5 large eggs, at room temperature
2 tablespoons unsalted butter or margarine
3 tablespoons all-purpose flour
1 cup low-fat milk
½ teaspoon salt
Pinch of Cayenne pepper
½ teaspoon Worcestershire sauce
¾ cup grated sharp Cheddar cheese
⅛ teaspoon cream of tartar

1. Preheat oven to 400 degrees. Generously butter and flour 2-quart soufflé dish, adding a buttered and floured aluminum foil collar if desired (see page 58 and illustration below).
2. Separate eggs, dropping 4 yolks into small bowl and reserving 1 yolk for another use; place 5 egg whites in large nonaluminum or glass bowl.
3. Melt butter or margarine in medium-size saucepan over medium heat. Add flour and cook, stirring constantly, 3 minutes, or until mixture is smooth. Do not allow mixture to brown.
4. Add milk and cook, whisking constantly, until sauce comes to a boil. Remove pan from heat.
5. Whisk in egg yolks one at a time. Add salt, Cayenne, and Worcestershire sauce, and whisk to combine.
6. Add cheese and stir until cheese is melted. Set cheese sauce aside.

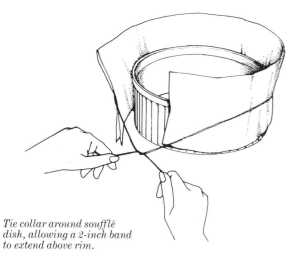

Tie collar around soufflé dish, allowing a 2-inch band to extend above rim.

7. Add cream of tartar to egg whites and beat with electric mixer at high speed until stiff but not dry. Stir one fourth of whites into cheese sauce. Gently fold in remaining whites. Do not overmix.
8. Spoon mixture into soufflé dish and place in oven. Reduce heat immediately to 375 degrees, and bake soufflé without opening oven door 20 minutes, or until puffed and lightly browned.
9. Carefully remove soufflé from oven, remove collar, and serve immediately.

Herbed Vegetables

2 large carrots (about ½ pound total weight)
2 medium-size zucchini (about 1 pound total weight)
Small head cauliflower
Small bunch fresh thyme, or 1 teaspoon dried
2 tablespoons unsalted butter or margarine
Salt
Freshly ground pepper

1. Wash carrots, zucchini, and cauliflower, and fresh thyme if using, and dry with paper towels. Trim carrots and zucchini. Cut enough carrots crosswise into ½-inch-thick slices to measure about 1 cup. Cut enough zucchini crosswise into ¼-inch-thick slices to measure about 3 cups. Trim stem and leaves from cauliflower and break enough cauliflower into small florets to measure about 2 cups. Reserve any remaining vegetables for another use. Mince enough fresh thyme to measure 1 tablespoon; reserve remaining thyme for another use. Or, if using dried thyme, crush in mortar with pestle or between fingers.
2. Bring 1 inch of water to a boil in large saucepan fitted with vegetable steamer.
3. Place carrots and cauliflower in vegetable steamer, cover pan, and cook 5 minutes, or until vegetables are crisp-tender. Turn vegetables into colander, refresh briefly under cold running water, and set aside to drain. Keep water in saucepan at a boil, adding hot water, if necessary, to maintain 1-inch level.
4. Place zucchini in steamer in saucepan and cook, covered, 3 minutes, or until crisp-tender. Refresh zucchini briefly under cold running water and turn into colander to drain.
5. Melt butter or margarine in large skillet over medium heat. Add thyme, vegetables, and salt and pepper to taste and cook, stirring, until heated through. Transfer vegetables to large serving bowl.

Arugula and Radicchio Salad with Warm Mushroom Dressing
Pasta Florentine
Braised Tomatoes

A summertime meal: cartwheel pasta with spinach and cheese, braised tomatoes, and mushrooms with arugula and radicchio.

The main dish calls for a cartwheel-shaped pasta some-times labeled *ruoti* or *rotelle*; if it is not available, any bite-size pasta is a good substitute.

For the salad, select fresh, domestic mushrooms that are pinkish-white and have tightly fitting caps that curve over the stems and cover the gills on the underside. Store the mushrooms for no more than two or three days in a loosely covered container in the refrigerator. If you cannot purchase arugula, use watercress instead.

WHAT TO DRINK

For a truly Florentine touch, serve a white Tuscan wine such as Galestro or Vernaccia di San Gimignano. If these are not available, a simple Soave or a light young Chianti would also be nice.

SHOPPING LIST AND STAPLES

2 small bunches arugula
Small head radicchio
½ pound fresh mushrooms
4 medium-size ripe tomatoes (about 3 pounds total weight)
Large onion
3 small cloves garlic
Small bunch fresh parsley
Small bunch fresh basil, or ½ teaspoon dried
Small lemon
¾ cup low-fat milk
½ pound part-skim mozzarella cheese
¼ pound Provolone cheese
¼ pound Parmesan cheese
2 ounces Romano cheese
10-ounce package frozen chopped spinach
2 tablespoons good-quality olive oil, preferably extra-virgin
2 tablespoons corn oil
½ cup red wine vinegar
2 teaspoons Dijon mustard
1 teaspoon Worcestershire sauce
½ pound cartwheel pasta or other bite-size pasta
2-ounce jar pine nuts
2 teaspoons sugar
1 teaspoon dried oregano
¼ teaspoon ground nutmeg
⅛ teaspoon ground allspice
Salt
Freshly ground white pepper
Freshly ground black pepper

UTENSILS

Food processor (optional)
Large skillet with cover
Large saucepan
Medium-size nonaluminum saucepan
2-quart casserole
Metal pie pan
Small bowl
Salad spinner (optional)
Colander
Strainer
Measuring cups and spoons
Chef's knife
Paring knife
Metal spatula
Wooden spoon
Slotted spoon
Grater (if not using food processor)
Citrus juicer (optional)
Small jar with tight-fitting lid
Mortar and pestle (optional)

START-TO-FINISH STEPS

1. Wash parsley and pat dry with paper towels. Finely chop enough parsley to measure 1 tablespoon for pasta recipe and 2 tablespoons for tomatoes recipe. Peel garlic and mince 1 clove for salad recipe and 2 cloves for tomatoes recipe.
2. Follow pasta recipe steps 1 through 3.
3. Follow tomatoes recipe steps 1 and 2.
4. While onion and garlic are cooking, follow pasta recipe step 4 and salad recipe steps 1 through 6.
5. Increase oven temperature to 450 degrees. Follow to-matoes recipe steps 3 through 5 and pasta recipe steps 5 through 8.
6. While pasta is baking, follow salad recipe steps 7 and 8.
7. Follow pasta recipe step 9, tomatoes recipe step 6, and serve with salad.

RECIPES

Arugula and Radicchio Salad with Warm Mushroom Dressing

2 small bunches arugula
Small head radicchio
Small lemon
½ pound fresh mushrooms
¼ cup pine nuts
¼ cup red wine vinegar
2 teaspoons sugar
1 teaspoon Worcestershire sauce
2 teaspoons Dijon mustard
Small clove garlic, minced
¼ teaspoon salt
⅛ teaspoon freshly ground black pepper
2 tablespoons good-quality olive oil, preferably extra-virgin

1. Preheat oven to 350 degrees.
2. Wash arugula and radicchio, separate into leaves, and dry in salad spinner or with paper towels.
3. Halve lemon. Squeeze enough juice from one half to measure 1 teaspoon. Reserve remaining half for another

use. Wipe mushrooms clean with damp paper towels and slice thinly.

4. Spread pine nuts in metal pie pan and toast in oven 5 minutes, or until lightly browned.

5. Meanwhile, in small jar with tight-fitting lid, combine lemon juice, vinegar, ¼ cup water, sugar, Worcestershire sauce, mustard, garlic, salt, and pepper. Add olive oil and shake vigorously.

6. Remove pine nuts from oven and set aside to cool.

7. Turn dressing into medium-size nonaluminum saucepan and heat over medium-high heat until hot. Add mushrooms and cook, stirring occasionally, 5 minutes, or until mushrooms are tender.

8. Divide radicchio leaves among 4 salad plates and top with arugula. Spoon mushrooms and dressing evenly over arugula and radicchio and sprinkle each salad with toasted pine nuts.

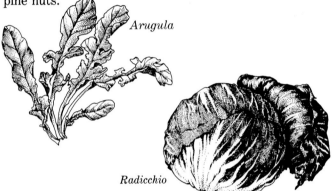

Arugula

Radicchio

Pasta Florentine

2 ounces Romano cheese
¼ pound Provolone cheese
½ pound part-skim mozzarella cheese
¼ pound Parmesan cheese
1 teaspoon dried oregano
10-ounce package frozen chopped spinach
½ pound cartwheel pasta or other bite-size pasta
½ teaspoon salt
¼ teaspoon ground nutmeg
¼ teaspoon freshly ground black pepper
¾ cup low-fat milk
1 tablespoon finely chopped parsley

1. Using food processor or grater, grate enough Romano to measure ½ cup; set aside.

2. Cut Provolone and mozzarella into ¼-inch cubes. Break or cut Parmesan into small pieces. You should have about 4½ cups total. Crush oregano in mortar with pestle or between fingers.

3. Thaw spinach in strainer under hot running water. Press spinach with back of spoon to remove excess moisture; set aside.

4. Bring 2 quarts water to a boil in large saucepan over high heat.

5. Cook pasta in boiling water according to package directions until *al dente*. Turn pasta into colander to drain, then return to saucepan.

6. Add salt, nutmeg, pepper, cubed cheeses, and spinach

to pasta and toss to combine well.

7. Oil 2-quart casserole. Turn pasta mixture into casserole. Pour in milk and sprinkle with Romano and parsley.

8. Bake pasta in preheated 450-degree oven about 10 minutes, or until bubbly and golden.

9. Divide pasta among 4 dinner plates.

Braised Tomatoes

4 medium-size ripe tomatoes (about 3 pounds total
    weight)
Small bunch fresh basil, or ½ teaspoon dried
Large onion
2 tablespoons corn oil
2 small cloves garlic, minced
⅛ teaspoon ground allspice
⅛ teaspoon salt
⅛ teaspoon freshly ground white pepper
¼ cup red wine vinegar
2 tablespoons finely chopped parsley

1. Wash tomatoes, and fresh basil if using, and dry with paper towels. Halve tomatoes through stem end, and core. Mince enough basil to measure 2 teaspoons. Or, if using dried basil, crush in mortar with pestle or between fingers. Peel onion and slice thinly.

2. Heat oil in large skillet over medium heat until hot. Reduce heat to low, add basil, onion, and garlic, and cook 10 minutes, or until onion is transparent.

3. Using slotted spoon, transfer mixture to small bowl.

4. Sprinkle cut sides of tomatoes with allspice, salt, and pepper. Place tomatoes, cut-sides down, in skillet and add ¼ cup water. Cover pan and cook tomatoes over medium heat 2 to 3 minutes, or until tender. Remove pan from heat. Using metal spatula, turn tomatoes cut-sides up.

5. Drizzle tomatoes with vinegar, top with onion mixture, and sprinkle with parsley. Let stand at room temperature until ready to serve.

6. To serve, divide tomatoes among 4 dinner plates.

ADDED TOUCH

This dessert is not only delicious, it is low in calories.

Bananas Amaretto

3 large bananas
3 tablespoons Amaretto liqueur
Small bunch mint for garnish (optional)

1. Peel bananas and slice thinly. Place in plastic bag and freeze until hard.

2. When hard, place bananas in food processor or blender with Amaretto and process until smooth. Spoon mixture into metal bowl and freeze, tightly covered, 2 to 3 hours or overnight.

3. Just before serving, wash mint, if using, and pat dry with paper towels. Cut 4 sprigs for garnish and reserve remainder for another use.

4. Scoop banana mixture into 4 sherbet glasses or goblets and garnish with mint, if desired.

John Robert Massie

MENU 1 (Right)
Creamy Peanut Soup
Pizza Crêpes with
Tomatoes, Zucchini, and Goat Cheese

MENU 2
Tomato Soup with Fresh Coriander
and Mozzarella
Artichokes with Wild Mushrooms and
Shirred Eggs

MENU 3
Vegetable Jambalaya
Sesame Green Beans with Hard-Boiled Eggs
Fruit Salad with Jalapeño-Lime Dressing

After years of cooking on the job every day, John Massie has learned to streamline the meals he prepares at home. He often turns to that old favorite, eggs, which he serves in many different ways. He finds that using fresh ingredients, including unusual herbs and seasonings, can elevate even the simplest dish. "When planning a meal, nutritional balance is naturally important," he says, "but without zest no dish is pleasing."

All three of his menus are inspired by his fondness for mixing cuisines—and all three use eggs. In Menu 1, East meets West: Individual egg "crêpes" are topped, pizza-style, with rounds of zucchini, tomatoes, and goat cheese, and are served with a Thai-inspired peanut soup. The soup includes coconut milk, cumin, coriander, and hot chilies in addition to peanuts and peanut butter.

Menu 2 is a satisfying and comforting meal with Italian and French overtones. It features a full-flavored soup made with three types of tomatoes: fresh, canned, and sun-dried. With the soup, the cook presents artichokes filled with creamed wild mushrooms and shirred eggs.

A particularly colorful brunch or buffet dinner, Menu 3 is an American-Oriental pairing of Creole-style vegetable jambalaya and green beans tossed with sesame oil. The beans, topped with chopped hard-boiled eggs and toasted sesame seeds, can be served as a first course, if desired. A tropical fruit salad sparked with minced jalapeños is the unusual dessert.

Let your guests garnish their bowls of creamy peanut soup with diced jalapeño peppers, scallions, tomatoes, peanuts, and wedges of lime. The Italian-inspired entrée features delicate egg "crêpes" topped with tomatoes, zucchini, and goat cheese.

Creamy Peanut Soup
Pizza Crêpes with Tomatoes, Zucchini, and Goat Cheese

The creamy peanut soup calls for a medley of unusual ingredients (both Oriental and Middle Eastern) including dried red chilies, coconut milk, and *tahini*. Dried red chilies are usually sold in cellophane packets or, occasionally, strung in long strands. Good-quality dried chilies will be of an even color, shiny, and unbroken. If stored in a cool dry place, they can last for several months; tightly sealed in a container and refrigerated or frozen, they will last indefinitely. As a substitute, you can use hot red pepper flakes: ¼ teaspoon equals one dried chili. Canned coconut milk (the cook suggests using a Thai brand) is made by steeping grated coconut meat in boiling water. Because this rich milk spoils quickly, after opening the can pour any leftover milk into a plastic container, seal it tightly, and freeze it. For information on *tahini* see page 78.

WHAT TO DRINK

A young and fruity red wine makes an ideal accompaniment for these dishes. Try a French Beaujolais—preferably from one of the named *crus*, such as Morgon or Juliénas—or an Italian Dolcetto or young California Zinfandel.

SHOPPING LIST AND STAPLES

4 ripe plum tomatoes (about ¾ pound total weight)
Medium-size firm, ripe tomato
Medium-size zucchini
Small bunch scallions
2 fresh jalapeño chilies, or 4-ounce can
Medium-size yellow onion
3 medium-size cloves garlic
Small bunch fresh thyme, or ¼ teaspoon dried
Large lime
4 eggs
2 teaspoons unsalted butter
11-ounce log chèvre, such as Montrachet
4 cups vegetable stock (see page 9), or 4 vegetable
  bouillon cubes, or 4 teaspoons tamari
2 tablespoons tahini
15-ounce can unsweetened coconut milk
1 cup creamy peanut butter
2 tablespoons good-quality olive oil, preferably extra-
  virgin

3 tablespoons vegetable oil
1 tablespoon all-purpose flour
½ cup dry roasted peanuts
3 dried red chili peppers
¼ teaspoon ground cumin
¼ teaspoon ground coriander
¼ teaspoon turmeric
Salt
Freshly ground black pepper

UTENSILS

Food processor (optional)
Small crêpe pan, or small skillet
Large nonaluminum saucepan
Small saucepan (optional)
Large baking sheet
Small bowl
Measuring cups and spoons
Chef's knife
Paring knife
Wooden spoon
Wide metal spatula
Rubber spatula
Whisk
Ladle
Mortar and pestle
Thin rubber gloves

START-TO-FINISH STEPS

1. Follow soup recipe steps 1 through 8.
2. Follow crêpes recipe steps 1 through 9.
3. Follow soup recipe step 9, crêpes recipe step 10, and serve.

RECIPES

Creamy Peanut Soup

4 cups vegetable stock (see page 9), or 4 vegetable
  bouillon cubes, or 4 teaspoons tamari
3 medium-size cloves garlic
Medium-size yellow onion
3 dried red chili peppers
3 tablespoons vegetable oil
1 tablespoon all-purpose flour

¼ teaspoon ground cumin
¼ teaspoon freshly ground black pepper
¼ teaspoon ground coriander
¼ teaspoon turmeric
2 tablespoons tahini
1 cup creamy peanut butter
½ cup canned unsweetened coconut milk
Large lime
Medium-size firm, ripe tomato
4 scallions
2 fresh or canned jalapeño chilies
½ cup dry roasted peanuts

1. If using bouillon cubes, bring 1 quart water to a boil in small saucepan over high heat. Add cubes and stir until dissolved. If using tamari, combine with 4 cups water. Set aside.
2. Peel garlic. Halve, peel, and quarter onion.
3. Using food processor or chef's knife, mince garlic and onion.
4. In large nonaluminum saucepan, sauté dried chilies in oil over medium-high heat 1 minute. Add garlic and onion and sauté, stirring frequently, about 5 minutes, or until golden but not dry.
5. Add flour, cumin, pepper, coriander, and turmeric, and cook, stirring constantly, 1 minute. Add vegetable stock, bouillon, or tamari mixture, and stir to combine. Bring to a boil.
6. Add tahini and peanut butter and stir until dissolved. Allow mixture to return to a boil.
7. Stir in coconut milk and boil until smooth, about 1 minute. Taste, and adjust seasonings if necessary. Keep soup warm over low heat.
8. For garnishes: Wash and dry lime, tomato, scallions, and jalapeños. Cut lime into 8 wedges. Halve, core, and seed tomato. Cut tomato into ½-inch cubes. Trim scallions and slice crosswise into thin rounds. Wearing rubber gloves, trim, halve, seed, and coarsely chop jalapeños. Coarsely chop peanuts. Place each garnish in separate small bowl.
9. To serve, ladle soup into 4 bowls and offer garnishes on the side.

Pizza Crêpes with Tomatoes, Zucchini, and Goat Cheese

11-ounce log chèvre, such as Montrachet
4 eggs

Salt
Freshly ground black pepper
2 teaspoons unsalted butter
Medium-size zucchini
4 ripe plum tomatoes (about ¾ pound total weight)
2 tablespoons good-quality olive oil, preferably extra-virgin
Small bunch fresh thyme, or ¼ teaspoon dried

1. Place chèvre in freezer to chill 10 minutes. Preheat broiler.
2. Break 1 egg into small bowl. Add 1 tablespoon cold water, a pinch of salt, and a pinch of freshly ground black pepper; whisk briefly to blend.
3. Melt ½ teaspoon butter in small crêpe pan or skillet over medium-high heat. Pour in beaten egg mixture and quickly rotate pan to make thin, even egg crêpe. Cook about 1 minute, or until egg is almost set but still slightly runny on top. Using wide metal spatula, carefully transfer crêpe, runny-side up, to large baking sheet. Wipe out pan and make 3 more crêpes, one at a time, with remaining eggs and butter, placing cooked crêpes side by side on baking sheet.
4. Wash and dry zucchini; trim ends but do not peel. Cut zucchini crosswise into ⅛-inch-thick rounds; set aside.
5. Wash and dry tomatoes; remove and discard stem ends. Slice tomatoes into ⅛-inch-thick rounds; set aside.
6. Using sharp knife dipped into very hot water, cut chèvre into 16 very thin rounds, wiping knife with damp paper towel after cutting each slice. If slices fall apart, they can be pieced together later. Crumble any remaining chèvre; set aside.
7. Arrange overlapping slices of zucchini, tomato, and chèvre in circular pattern on each crêpe. Fill center of crêpe with crumbled goat cheese, if desired.
8. Sprinkle top of each crêpe with about 1½ teaspoons olive oil. If using fresh thyme, remove 4 small sprigs from stems; wash and pat dry. Remove leaves from sprigs and chop coarsely. If using dried thyme, crush in mortar with pestle. Or, crush between fingers. Sprinkle crêpes with chopped or crushed thyme, and season with salt and black pepper to taste.
9. Broil crêpes 4 inches from heat 3 to 4 minutes, or until cheese bubbles and vegetables begin to wilt.
10. With wide metal spatula, carefully transfer crêpes to 4 dinner plates and serve.

Tomato Soup with Fresh Coriander and Mozzarella
Artichokes with Wild Mushrooms and Shirred Eggs

For a warming meal, serve bowls of rich tomato soup with mozzarella and coriander, and egg-and-mushroom-filled artichokes.

Stuffed artichokes make an elegant accompaniment to the tomato soup. In the final cooking phase, the savory mushroom sauce seeps down into the artichoke leaves. A component of the sauce is *crème fraîche*, a silky-textured cultivated cream product resembling sour cream. *Crème fraîche* is expensive, and not readily available even in well-stocked dairy departments. You can substitute sour cream, or make your own *crème fraîche* in advance: Whisk ½ pint heavy cream into ½ pint sour cream at room temperature. Pour this mixture into a glass jar, cover it tightly, and let it stand in a warm place for 6 to 8 hours, then refrigerate. It will keep, refrigerated, for 10 days.

WHAT TO DRINK

Artichokes are difficult to match with any wine. Your best bet is a flavorful, acidic white, such as a California Sauvignon Blanc or a French Sancerre or Pouilly-Fumé.

SHOPPING LIST AND STAPLES

2 medium-size ripe tomatoes (about ¾ pound total weight)
4 large artichokes (each about ¾ pound)
1 pound fresh cèpes, porcini, or large white mushrooms
Medium-size onion
3 medium-size cloves garlic
Small bunch fresh coriander, preferably with roots attached
Small bunch fresh parsley
Small lemon
4 eggs
1 pint heavy cream
1 cup crème fraîche, homemade (see above) or commercial
4 tablespoons unsalted butter
1 ounce Parmesan cheese
2 ounces fresh mozzarella
35-ounce can Italian plum tomatoes
6½-ounce jar oil-packed sun-dried tomatoes
2 tablespoons good-quality olive oil, preferably extra-virgin
Salt
Freshly ground black pepper
¼ cup Cognac

UTENSILS

Food processor or blender
Large heavy-gauge nonaluminum sauté pan
Large heavy-gauge nonaluminum saucepan
Large saucepan with cover
Large vegetable steamer
Large baking sheet
Fine strainer
Measuring cups and spoons
Chef's knife
Paring knife
Wooden spoon
Rubber spatula
Grater
Citrus juicer (optional)
Melon baller (optional)
Ladle
Kitchen shears (optional)

START-TO-FINISH STEPS

1. Follow soup recipe steps 1 through 3.
2. While soup is cooking, follow artichokes recipe steps 1 through 9.
3. Follow soup recipe steps 4 and 5.
4. Follow artichokes recipe steps 10 through 13 and soup recipe step 6.
5. Follow artichokes recipe step 14, soup recipe step 7, and serve.

RECIPES

Tomato Soup with Fresh Coriander and Mozzarella

Medium-size onion
3 medium-size cloves garlic
2 medium-size ripe tomatoes (about ¾ pound total weight)
Small bunch fresh coriander, preferably with roots attached
2 tablespoons good-quality olive oil, preferably extra-virgin
35-ounce can Italian plum tomatoes
6 oil-packed sun-dried tomatoes
2 ounces fresh mozzarella
Salt and freshly ground black pepper

1. Peel onion and thinly slice enough to measure about 1 cup. Peel garlic and thinly slice enough to measure about 1 tablespoon. Wash and dry fresh tomatoes; remove and discard stem ends. Quarter tomatoes. Wash coriander, carefully cleaning roots, and pat dry. Remove 8 whole sprigs coriander and set aside for garnish. Strip leaves from remaining stems. Set aside stems and roots; reserve leaves for another use.
2. Heat oil in large heavy-gauge nonaluminum saucepan over medium heat. Add onion and garlic and sauté about 5 minutes, or until translucent.
3. Add fresh tomatoes, coriander roots and stems, canned tomatoes with their juice, and sun-dried tomatoes to saucepan. Increase heat to high and bring mixture to a boil, stirring occasionally with wooden spoon to break up tomatoes. Reduce heat to medium-high and boil gently about 30 minutes, stirring occasionally.
4. Remove soup from heat and set aside to cool slightly.
5. Meanwhile, finely shred mozzarella and set aside until needed.
6. Ladle soup into container of food processor or blender

and purée until very smooth. Strain soup through fine strainer back into saucepan. If soup seems very thick, dilute with water to desired consistency. Add salt and pepper to taste. Keep soup hot over low heat until ready to serve.

7. Ladle soup into 4 bowls. Divide mozzarella among bowls and garnish each bowl with 2 sprigs coriander.

Artichokes with Wild Mushrooms and Shirred Eggs

4 large artichokes (each about ¾ pound)
1 pound fresh cèpes, porcini, or large white mushrooms
4 tablespoons unsalted butter
Salt and freshly ground black pepper
¼ cup Cognac
2 cups heavy cream
1 cup crème fraîche
Small lemon
1 ounce Parmesan cheese
4 eggs
Small bunch parsley

1. Preheat oven to 400 degrees.
2. In saucepan large enough to accommodate large vegetable steamer, bring 2 cups water to a boil over medium heat.
3. Meanwhile, prepare artichokes: Snap off stems near base; pare base so artichoke will sit upright. Holding artichoke horizontally against cutting board, cut off top inch of leaves. If desired, snip off pointed ends of remaining leaves. Holding artichokes under cold running water, gently spread leaves, exposing shiny, purple petals in center. Using melon baller or teaspoon, carefully remove small petals and fuzzy choke immediately underneath, removing as little of heart as possible.
4. Place artichokes upside down in steamer over boiling water. Cover pan tightly and steam about 15 minutes, or until stem end is tender when pierced with a knife tip.
5. Meanwhile, trim, wash, and drain cèpes or porcini. If using white mushrooms, wipe clean with damp paper towels. Cut mushrooms into ¼-inch-wide strips.
6. Melt butter in large heavy-gauge nonaluminum sauté pan over medium-high heat. Add mushrooms, a pinch of salt, and a pinch of pepper, and sauté about 6 minutes, or until mushrooms release their moisture.
7. Remove pan from heat. Add Cognac and, averting your face, carefully ignite. When flames subside, stir in heavy cream and crème fraîche and cook over medium heat, being careful not to let mixture boil over, about 15 minutes, or until mushrooms are tender and liquid is thick.
8. Halve lemon and squeeze enough juice to measure 4 teaspoons. Finely grate enough Parmesan to measure 2 tablespoons; set aside.
9. Remove artichokes from steamer and place upright on large baking sheet.
10. Gently spread artichoke leaves open. Sprinkle cavity of each artichoke with 1 teaspoon lemon juice, and season with a pinch of salt and pepper. Divide mushrooms and

their sauce among artichoke cavities, filling each almost to the top.
11. Break 1 egg over filling in each artichoke. Yolk should remain on top; egg white will run between leaves. Sprinkle each artichoke with 1½ teaspoons Parmesan.
12. Bake artichokes about 10 minutes, or until eggs are gently set.
13. Meanwhile, wash and dry parsley. Set aside 4 sprigs for garnish and reserve remainder for another use.
14. Divide artichokes among 4 dinner plates and garnish each with a parsley sprig.

ADDED TOUCH

This simple yet elegant tart makes a spectacular offering with its puffy crust and glazed-apple filling.

Apple Tart

¼ pound frozen puff pastry, thawed
2 small Golden Delicious apples
3 tablespoons sugar
2 tablespoons unsalted butter
1 egg
Pinch of salt
¼ cup apricot jam
1 tablespoon Cognac
1 cup crème fraîche (optional)

1. Line large baking sheet with parchment paper. Place puff pastry on parchment and roll out to ⅛ inch thick.
2. Using inverted cake pan as a guide, cut 8-inch round from pastry. Reserve pastry scraps for another use.
3. Using sharp knife, without cutting completely through pastry, carefully score a circle ½ inch inside edge of pastry round to make a border. Prick inner circle of pastry round with fork about every inch to prevent it from rising.
4. Peel and core apples. Halve apples through stem ends and lay each half flat on cutting surface. Slice each half lengthwise as thinly as possible, keeping each half intact.
5. Sprinkle 1 tablespoon sugar over inner circle of pastry round. Using wide metal spatula, carefully transfer sliced apple halves to inner circle of pastry round. Fan out apple slices slightly, keeping fruit within and not touching border, which must be kept free to rise as tart bakes.
6. Sprinkle apples with remaining 2 tablespoons sugar. Cut butter into bits. Dot each apple half with about 1½ teaspoons butter. Refrigerate tart 30 minutes.
7. Preheat oven to 375 degrees.
8. In small bowl, lightly beat egg with salt. With pastry brush, lightly brush outer circle of tart with beaten egg.
9. Bake tart on middle rack of preheated oven about 35 minutes, or until border is well browned and apples are tender when pierced with knife.
10. Meanwhile, in small saucepan melt apricot jam with Cognac over medium heat. Strain jam mixture into second saucepan and keep warm on stove top.
11. Remove tart from oven and while still hot, brush apples and crust with apricot glaze. Cut tart into wedges and serve warm, with crème fraîche, if desired.

Vegetable Jambalaya
Sesame Green Beans with Hard-Boiled Eggs
Fruit Salad with Jalapeño-Lime Dressing

The interplay of spicy, pungent, and sweet flavors marks this meal of vegetable jambalaya, beans in sesame oil, and fruit salad.

A classic Creole dish, jambalaya is usually a combination of meat, shellfish, vegetables, rice, and a variety of seasonings. In this all-vegetable version okra is a prime ingredient. This tapered green or white seed pod exudes a thick liquid during cooking that gives substance to the stew. Buy tender pods no more than 4 inches long that snap easily; larger pods may be slightly woody.

As alternatives to homemade vegetable stock, the cook suggests vegetable bouillon cubes or 2 tablespoons of *tamari,* mixed with water. Look for preservative-free bouillon cubes; some brands are also available in salt-free form. *Tamari* is a richly flavored, naturally brewed soy sauce, available in Oriental markets and health food stores.

WHAT TO DRINK

Cold beer or ale is a natural choice for this menu. If you prefer wine, try a well-chilled Gewürztraminer from Alsace or California.

SHOPPING LIST AND STAPLES

1 pound green beans
Large green bell pepper
Large red bell pepper
Small bunch celery
½ pound fresh okra, or 10-ounce package frozen sliced okra
Large bunch scallions
Small fresh jalapeño chili
Large yellow onion
3 medium-size cloves garlic
Small bunch mint
Small ripe pineapple (about 3 pounds)
Small ripe papaya, or 1 pint strawberries
Medium-size ripe pear
Medium-size ripe banana
Medium-size ripe peach
Large lime
4 eggs
3 tablespoons unsalted butter

2 cups vegetable stock (see page 9), or 2 vegetable
    bouillon cubes, or 2 teaspoons tamari
16-ounce can Italian plum tomatoes
¼ cup Oriental sesame oil
1 tablespoon vegetable oil
3-ounce bottle Louisiana-style hot sauce
1½ cups converted long-grain white rice
1 cup blanched or raw peanuts (about 6 ounces)
1 tablespoon plus 1 teaspoon sesame seeds
1 teaspoon hot paprika
1 teaspoon dried thyme
1 teaspoon dried oregano
½ teaspoon Cayenne pepper
3 bay leaves
Salt
Freshly ground black pepper

<hr>

UTENSILS

Small skillet
Large saucepan
Medium-size saucepan with cover
Small saucepan (optional)
Large flameproof casserole with cover
2 large bowls, 1 nonaluminum
Colander
Measuring cups and spoons
Chef's knife
Paring knife
Wooden spoon
Slotted spoon
Citrus juicer (optional)
Vegetable peeler (optional)
Thin rubber gloves

<hr>

START-TO-FINISH STEPS

One hour ahead: If using frozen okra for jambalaya recipe, set out 1½ cups to thaw.

1. Follow green beans recipe steps 1 and 2 and jambalaya recipe steps 1 and 2.
2. Follow green beans recipe step 3.
3. While beans are cooking, follow fruit salad recipe step 1.
4. Follow green beans recipe steps 4 and 5.
5. Follow jambalaya recipe step 3 and green beans recipe step 6.

6. Follow jambalaya recipe steps 4 and 5.
7. While jambalaya is cooking, follow green beans recipe step 7 and fruit salad recipe steps 2 and 3.
8. Follow jambalaya recipe step 6 and fruit salad recipe steps 4 through 7.
9. Follow jambalaya recipe steps 7 and 8 and serve with green beans.
10. Follow fruit salad recipe step 8 and serve for dessert.

<hr>

RECIPES

Vegetable Jambalaya

2 cups vegetable stock, or 2 vegetable bouillon cubes, or 2
    teaspoons tamari
Large yellow onion
3 medium-size cloves garlic
Large green bell pepper
Large red bell pepper
3 stalks celery
Large bunch scallions
½ pound fresh okra, or 1½ cups frozen sliced okra,
    thawed
3 tablespoons unsalted butter
16-ounce can Italian plum tomatoes
3 bay leaves
2 tablespoons Louisiana-style hot sauce
1 teaspoon hot paprika
1 teaspoon dried thyme
1 teaspoon dried oregano
½ teaspoon Cayenne pepper
½ teaspoon freshly ground black pepper
2 teaspoons salt
1½ cups converted long-grain white rice
1 cup blanched or raw peanuts

1. If using vegetable bouillon cubes, bring 2 cups water to a boil in small saucepan over high heat. Dissolve cubes in water and set aside. If using tamari, stir into 2 cups water and set aside.
2. Peel onion and coarsely chop enough to measure about 1½ cups. Peel and mince garlic. Wash green and red bell peppers, celery, scallions, and fresh okra and dry with paper towels. Halve, core, seed, and coarsely chop enough peppers to measure about 3 cups combined. Trim celery and coarsely chop enough to measure about 1½ cups. Trim scallions and thinly slice enough white and green parts to measure about 1 cup. Trim stem ends of okra. Cut enough

okra crosswise into ½-inch-thick slices to measure about 1½ cups.

3. Melt butter in large flameproof casserole over medium-high heat. Add onion, garlic, bell peppers, and celery, and sauté, stirring frequently, 5 minutes, or until vegetables begin to soften.

4. Add vegetable stock, bouillon mixture, or tamari mixture, plum tomatoes and their juice, bay leaves, hot sauce, paprika, thyme, oregano, Cayenne, black pepper, and salt. Bring mixture to a boil, stirring frequently. Partially cover pan, reduce heat to medium-low, and simmer 5 minutes.

5. Stir in rice and peanuts and simmer jambalaya, partially covered, another 10 minutes.

6. Stir in scallions and fresh or frozen okra and cook, partially covered, another 10 minutes, or until rice is tender.

7. Taste jambalaya, and add salt, pepper, Cayenne, or hot sauce, if necessary; jambalaya should be very spicy. Remove and discard bay leaves.

8. Turn jambalaya into serving dish, or serve directly from casserole.

Sesame Green Beans with Hard-Boiled Eggs

4 eggs
1 pound green beans
¼ cup Oriental sesame oil
1 tablespoon plus 1 teaspoon sesame seeds
Freshly ground black pepper

1. Place eggs in medium-size saucepan and add cold water to cover. Bring water to a boil over high heat. Remove pan from heat, tightly cover pan, and set aside 20 minutes.

2. Meanwhile, bring large saucepan of water to a boil over high heat. Wash beans and trim ends.

3. Drop beans into boiling water. When water returns to a boil, cook beans about 5 minutes, or until tender.

4. Drain beans in colander, refresh under cold running water, and drain on paper towels.

5. In large bowl, toss beans with sesame oil. With slotted spoon, transfer beans but not oil to serving bowl and set aside.

6. Cool eggs under cold running water; peel and rinse. Coarsely chop eggs and sprinkle over beans.

7. Toast sesame seeds in small skillet over moderate heat, tossing frequently, 1 to 2 minutes, or until golden. Sprinkle beans and eggs with sesame seeds and season with

freshly ground black pepper to taste. Set beans aside at room temperature until ready to serve.

Fruit Salad with Jalapeño-Lime Dressing

Small fresh jalapeño chili
Large lime
1 tablespoon vegetable oil
Small bunch mint
Salt
Freshly ground black pepper
Small ripe pineapple (about 3 pounds)
Small ripe papaya, or 1 pint strawberries
Medium-size ripe pear
Medium-size ripe banana
Medium-size ripe peach

1. Wash jalapeño, and wearing rubber gloves, halve jalapeño lengthwise and remove stem and seeds. Finely mince jalapeño and place in large nonaluminum bowl.

2. Halve lime and squeeze enough juice to measure 2 tablespoons. Add lime juice and vegetable oil to jalapeño. Wash mint and pat dry. Set aside 4 mint sprigs for garnish and mince enough remaining mint to measure 1 tablespoon. Add minced mint, a pinch of salt, and about ⅛ teaspoon freshly ground black pepper to dressing. Stir to blend well; set aside.

3. Using chef's knife, cut off top and bottom of pineapple. Pare pineapple, starting from top and cutting downward. Cut deeply enough to remove the eyes. Halve pineapple lengthwise; reserve one half for another use. Cut remaining half lengthwise into 3 pieces; remove and discard cores. Cut pieces crosswise into ½-inch chunks and add to bowl with dressing.

4. Peel papaya if using, halve lengthwise, and scoop out seeds. Cut flesh into 1-inch chunks and add to bowl. Or, if using strawberries, wash, hull, and halve berries; add to bowl.

5. Halve and core pear. Cut lengthwise into ½-inch-thick slices; add to bowl.

6. Peel banana and cut crosswise into ½-inch-thick slices; add to bowl.

7. Peel and halve peach and discard pit. Slice peach lengthwise into ½-inch-thick slices; add to bowl. Toss fruit to coat with dressing. Set fruit salad aside at room temperature until ready to serve.

8. To serve, garnish salad with mint sprigs.

Hidehiko Takada and Ursula Forem

MENU 1 (Right)
Watercress Rolls
Curried Vegetable Stew
Steamed Rice

MENU 2
Vegetable Salad with Tofu-Tahini Dressing
Egg Crêpes with Mushrooms and Bean Sprouts
Soba Noodles with Peanut Sauce and Spinach

MENU 3
Broiled Eggplant with Miso Sauce
Pan-Fried Tofu with Vegetables
Sweet and Sour Rice

Cooking collaborators Hidehiko Takada and Ursula Forem have a common goal—to teach Americans that Japanese meals are not only healthful and attractive but easy to prepare. They believe that choosing a meatless diet need not limit one to the bland and boring. For these menus they have created a number of versatile vegetable dishes that are equally good for lunch, brunch, or dinner.

The tempting noodle dish of Menu 2, cold *soba* sauced with an artful blend of peanut butter, honey, and vinegar, and topped with spinach, can be made well in advance of serving. It is presented with tender egg crêpes filled with mushrooms, bean sprouts, and onions, and is preceded by a vegetable salad.

These two cooks also want Americans to realize that Japanese food is more than *sushi* and *tempura*, as their hearty stew in Menu 1 readily shows. This robust vegetable dish is seasoned with curry, a spice usually associated with Indian cooking, which is, in fact, quite popular in Japan. In addition to vegetables the stew includes nuts and beans.

The entrée of Menu 3 features tofu, or bean curd, a versatile food high in protein. Here the tofu is pan-fried to a golden brown, surrounded by crisp-tender vegetables, and topped with a savory sauce. Broiled eggplant halves with miso sauce and sweet and sour rice accompany the tofu dish.

Delicate watercress-filled egg crêpes are a delightful contrast to the hearty curried vegetable stew and steamed sweet rice. The flavor of the stew intensifies if it is made the day before serving and refrigerated.

Watercress Rolls
Curried Vegetable Stew
Steamed Rice

The curried vegetable stew is a warming dish for a cold day. The amount of curry powder can be adjusted to suit your taste but the seasoning should remain subtle to preserve the delicate flavors of the vegetables.

Ideally, the stew should be served with Japanese sweet, or glutinous, rice. This short-grain rice (*kome* in Japanese) is moist and sticky when cooked. *Kome* is readily available in Oriental markets and many supermarkets and may be labeled "Japanese Rose" or "California Rose." Store it in an airtight container in a cool, dry place for up to six months. Short-grain rice requires thorough rinsing to remove excess starch but needs less water for cooking than medium- or long-grain rice. The cooks recommend using an automatic rice cooker, an electric pot that simultaneously steams and boils the grains to produce moister rice. Follow the manufacturer's directions if using an automatic cooker. See page 103 for mail-ordering sweet rice.

WHAT TO DRINK

The cooks recommend beer with the curry stew; a Japanese or Indian brand would be ideal. If you would rather have wine, a Soave would be good. Japanese green tea is appropriate afterward.

SHOPPING LIST AND STAPLES

1 pound potatoes
½ pound carrots
16 small mushrooms
Medium-size bunch watercress (about 6 ounces)
Large onion
6 large eggs
2 tablespoons unsalted butter
4 cups vegetable or chicken stock, preferably homemade (see page 9)
10-ounce package frozen peas, or 1 cup shelled fresh peas
16-ounce can white kidney beans
4 teaspoons vegetable oil
2 tablespoons Japanese soy sauce
1½ cups Japanese sweet rice
¼ cup cashews
2 tablespoons sugar
2 tablespoons cornstarch
2 tablespoons curry powder, approximately
Salt
2 tablespoons mirin or sweet cooking wine

UTENSILS

Large stockpot
Medium-size stockpot
8-inch nonstick skillet
Medium-size heavy-gauge saucepan with cover
2 medium-size bowls
2 small bowls
Salad spinner (optional)
Large strainer
Measuring cups and spoons
Chef's knife
Paring knife
Nylon spatula
Wooden spoon
Whisk
Basting brush
Vegetable peeler (optional)

START-TO-FINISH STEPS

1. Follow watercress rolls recipe steps 1 and 2 and rice recipe step 1.
2. Follow stew recipe steps 1 through 3.
3. Follow watercress rolls recipe step 3.
4. Follow stew recipe steps 4 and 5 and rice recipe step 2.
5. Follow stew recipe step 6 and rice recipe step 3.
6. Follow stew recipe step 7 and rice recipe step 4.
7. While stew and rice cook, follow watercress rolls recipe steps 4 through 7.
8. Follow rice recipe step 5 and stew recipe steps 8 and 9.
9. Follow rice recipe step 6 and stew recipe step 10, and serve with watercress rolls.

RECIPES

Watercress Rolls

Medium-size bunch watercress (about 6 ounces)
2 tablespoons sugar
2 tablespoons mirin or sweet cooking wine
6 large eggs
4 teaspoons vegetable oil

1. Fill medium-size stockpot half full of water and bring to a boil over high heat.
2. Meanwhile, wash watercress and dry in salad spinner or with paper towels. Remove and discard tough stems.

3. Plunge watercress into boiling water and blanch 1 to 1½ minutes, or until just wilted. Turn watercress into large strainer and refresh under cold running water. Squeeze watercress gently to remove excess water and spread on paper towels to drain.

4. Combine sugar and mirin in medium-size bowl. In another medium-size bowl, whisk eggs until frothy. Strain eggs into mirin mixture. Lightly whisk eggs and mirin mixture together.

5. Heat 8-inch nonstick skillet over medium heat until hot. Reduce heat to medium-low and brush skillet with 1 teaspoon oil. Pour in one fourth of egg mixture and tilt skillet to distribute mixture evenly over bottom of pan. Cook 1 minute, or until egg appears almost dry. Loosen edges with nylon spatula, carefully flip egg crêpe over, and cook another 10 seconds. Transfer to large sheet of waxed paper. Make 3 more egg crêpes with remaining oil and egg mixture. Do not stack.

6. Spread one fourth of watercress along bottom edge of one crêpe and roll up crêpe jelly-roll fashion. Repeat procedure with remaining crêpes and watercress.

7. Cut each roll crosswise into 4 pieces, each about 1½ inches long, and place on serving platter. Set aside at room temperature until ready to serve.

Curried Vegetable Stew

½ pound carrots
1 pound potatoes
Large onion
16 small mushrooms
1 cup white kidney beans
2 tablespoons cornstarch
4 cups vegetable or chicken stock
1½ to 2 tablespoons curry powder
2 tablespoons unsalted butter
10-ounce package frozen peas, or 1 cup
   shelled fresh peas
¼ cup cashews
2 tablespoons Japanese soy sauce
¼ teaspoon salt, approximately

1. Peel and trim carrots. Cut on diagonal into 1½-inch-long pieces; you should have about 2 cups. Peel potatoes and cut into 1½-inch chunks; you should have about 3 cups. Peel onion and cut into 1½-inch chunks; you should have about 1¼ cups.

2. Wipe mushrooms clean with damp paper towels. Turn beans into strainer, rinse, and drain.

3. Dissolve cornstarch in ¼ cup stock in small bowl. In another small bowl, combine curry powder and 1 tablespoon water to form a paste.

4. Melt butter in large stockpot over medium-high heat. Add carrots, potatoes, and onion, and cook, stirring occasionally, 3 to 4 minutes, or until well coated with butter.

5. Meanwhile, if using frozen peas, set aside 1 cup. Return remaining peas to freezer for another use.

6. Add remaining 3¾ cups stock to stockpot, increase heat to high, and bring to a boil.

7. Reduce heat to medium-low and cook at a low boil about 15 minutes, or until vegetables are tender.

8. Add mushrooms, beans, peas, and cashews to vegetables. Stir in curry paste, soy sauce, and salt to taste and continue to cook over medium-low heat 2 to 3 minutes.

9. Reduce heat so stew is at a simmer and slowly stir in cornstarch mixture. Cook, stirring, 1 minute, or until stew is just thickened. Simmer over very low heat, stirring occasionally, another 10 minutes.

10. Divide stew among 4 individual bowls.

Steamed Rice

1½ cups Japanese sweet rice

1. Place rice in medium-size heavy-gauge saucepan. Rinse under cold running water, drain, and repeat 3 or 4 times to remove surface starch from rice. (Water will be milky in color at first and after several rinses will become almost clear.) Turn rice into strainer to drain. When drained, return rice to pan and add 1½ cups water; set aside.

2. Cover pan and cook rice over high heat 5 minutes, or until it begins to steam.

3. Reduce heat to medium-low and cook another 7 minutes.

4. Reduce heat to low and cook another 13 minutes.

5. Remove pan from heat and let rice stand, covered, at least 15 minutes.

6. Divide rice among 4 dinner plates.

_____

ADDED TOUCH

The dressing for the cucumber salad calls for two common Japanese products: *mirin* and rice vinegar. A sweet, syrupy cooking wine made from glutinous rice, *mirin* is used for seasoning many Japanese dishes. You can make your own *mirin* by briefly simmering equal parts of *sake* and sugar together in a small saucepan. Rice vinegar is lighter and milder than Western-style vinegars. If you cannot find it, substitute apple cider vinegar.

Cucumber Salad with Rice Vinegar Dressing

2 kirby cucumbers
Small lemon
½ cup rice vinegar
2 tablespoons Japanese soy sauce
1 tablespoon sugar
1 tablespoon mirin or sweet cooking wine

1. Wash cucumbers and lemon and dry with paper towels. Using vegetable peeler, pare cucumbers lengthwise to create stripes of green and white. Cut cucumbers crosswise into ⅛-inch-thick slices. Halve lemon and cut one half into 4 wedges, reserving remaining half for another use.

2. Combine vinegar, soy sauce, sugar, and mirin in small bowl and stir until sugar dissolves.

3. Divide cucumber slices among 4 small plates and pour dressing equally over each salad. Garnish each salad with a lemon wedge and serve.

Vegetable Salad with Tofu-Tahini Dressing
Egg Crêpes with Mushrooms and Bean Sprouts
Soba Noodles with Peanut Sauce and Spinach

Of the many varieties of noodles eaten in Japan, one of the most popular is the thin gray-brown buckwheat noodle known as *soba*. Many Japanese restaurants and street vendors offer noodles exclusively—served hot in broth or cold with a dipping sauce. In this country *soba* noodles are readily available in Japanese markets and health food stores, but if you cannot find them, use a good-quality spaghetti instead.

Preparing the tender egg crêpes may seem difficult but is surprisingly easy. For success, heat a nonstick pan until hot, grease it, and then carefully pour in the beaten egg so it flows over the bottom of the pan. The cooked crêpes are fragile, but if you use a wide spatula, they will slide out of the pan easily.

The dressing for the salad calls for *tahini*, a Middle Eastern sesame paste made from ground, hulled, untoasted sesame seeds. *Tahini* is available in Middle Eastern markets, health food stores, and specialty food shops. Do not substitute Oriental sesame paste, which has a stronger flavor. The cooks also suggest using silken tofu, a type of tofu with a particularly smooth, soft texture and a subtle flavor. It is available at most Oriental markets.

WHAT TO DRINK

Hot tea or warm sake is a traditional beverage with these dishes.

SHOPPING LIST AND STAPLES

¼ pound tofu, preferably silken
1 pound spinach
¾ pound large mushrooms
4-ounce package enoki mushrooms
Small head romaine lettuce
Small head red cabbage
1 cup fresh mung bean sprouts (about 4 ounces)
Large onion
Small bunch parsley (optional)
Large orange
Large lemon
5 eggs
2 tablespoons unsalted butter
4 teaspoons vegetable oil
2 tablespoons Oriental sesame oil
2 tablespoons tahini
½ cup creamy peanut butter

A colorful tossed salad with tofu-tahini dressing, egg crêpes stuffed with mushrooms, bean sprouts, and onions, and cold soba noodles in a creamy peanut sauce make a satisfying meal for family and friends.

1 tablespoon honey
1 tablespoon rice vinegar or apple cider vinegar
½ cup Japanese soy sauce, approximately
3 tablespoons Worcestershire sauce, approximately
½ cup mayonnaise
2 tablespoons ketchup
1 teaspoon spicy prepared mustard
½ pound soba noodles or good-quality spaghetti
4 teaspoons sugar
Freshly ground pepper
½ cup mirin or sweet cooking wine, approximately

UTENSILS

Food processor or blender
Large stockpot
8-inch nonstick skillet
Large skillet with cover
Large ovenproof platter
5 small bowls
Strainer
Colander
Salad spinner (optional)
Measuring cups and spoons
Chef's knife
Paring knife
Nylon spatula
Rubber spatula
Wooden spoon
Citrus juicer (optional)
Whisk
Pastry brush

START-TO-FINISH STEPS

1. Follow salad recipe steps 1 through 4.
2. Follow noodles recipe steps 1 through 5 and crêpes recipe steps 1 and 2.
3. Follow noodles recipe step 6 and crêpes recipe steps 3 through 7.
4. Follow salad recipe step 5 and serve as first course.
5. Follow noodles recipe step 7, crêpes recipe step 8, and serve.

RECIPES

Vegetable Salad with Tofu-Tahini Dressing

Small head romaine lettuce
Small head red cabbage
4-ounce package enoki mushrooms
Large lemon
2 tablespoons tahini
2 tablespoons mirin or sweet cooking wine, approximately
1 teaspoon Worcestershire sauce
¼ pound tofu, preferably silken
1 teaspoon sugar

2 teaspoons Japanese soy sauce
¼ teaspoon freshly ground pepper

1. Wash romaine and dry in salad spinner or with paper towels; discard any bruised or discolored leaves. Tear romaine into bite-size pieces. Wash, dry, halve, and core cabbage. Shred enough cabbage to measure about 2 cups. Reserve remaining cabbage for another use. Trim mushroom stems.
2. Halve lemon and squeeze enough juice to measure 3 to 4 tablespoons.
3. Combine tahini, 2 tablespoons mirin, and 2 tablespoons water in container of food processor or blender and process until blended. Add Worcestershire sauce and tofu and process until smooth. Add 3 tablespoons lemon juice, sugar, soy sauce, and pepper, and processs until smooth. (Thin with additional mirin or lemon juice if desired.)
4. Transfer dressing to small bowl and set aside until needed.
5. Just before serving, pour dressing over vegetables and toss to coat. Divide vegetables among 4 salad plates.

Egg Crêpes with Mushrooms and Bean Sprouts

Large onion
¾ pound large mushrooms
1 cup fresh mung bean sprouts (about 4 ounces)
Small bunch parsley (optional)
½ cup mayonnaise
2 tablespoons ketchup
1½ tablespoons Worcestershire sauce
2 tablespoons unsalted butter
2 tablespoons Japanese soy sauce
2 tablespoons Oriental sesame oil
¼ teaspoon freshly ground pepper
1 tablespoon sugar
1 tablespoon mirin or sweet cooking wine
4 eggs
4 teaspoons vegetable oil

1. Peel onion and cut enough into ⅛-inch-thick slices to measure about 1 cup. Wipe mushrooms clean with damp paper towels and cut enough into ⅛-inch-thick slices to measure about 4 cups. Turn bean sprouts into strainer; rinse under cold running water and drain. Pat sprouts dry with paper towels and set aside. Wash parsley, if using, and dry with paper towels. Set aside 4 sprigs for garnish; reserve remaining parsley for another use.
2. For sauce, combine mayonnaise, ketchup, and Worcestershire sauce in small bowl; set aside until needed.
3. Preheat oven to 200 degrees.
4. For filling, heat butter in large skillet over medium heat. When foam subsides, add onion and cook, stirring occasionally, 2 minutes, or until onion is translucent. Add mushrooms and bean sprouts and cook 3 minutes, or until onion is golden brown. Add soy sauce, sesame oil, and pepper, and stir to combine. Remove skillet from heat.
5. Whisk together sugar, mirin, and eggs in small bowl.

6. Heat 8-inch nonstick skillet over medium heat until hot; brush skillet with 1 teaspoon oil. Pour in one fourth of egg mixture and tilt skillet to distribute mixture evenly over bottom of pan. Cook, breaking any bubbles as they form, 1 to 2 minutes, or until egg appears almost dry. Using nylon spatula, transfer crêpe to large ovenproof platter. Make 3 more crêpes with remaining oil and egg mixture, placing each on platter. Do not stack crêpes.

7. Divide filling among crêpes, leaving bottom third of each crêpe uncovered. Fold up bottom third and fold in sides, one over the other, to enclose filling on three sides. Place crêpes in 200-degree oven to keep warm.

8. Just before serving, spoon some sauce over each crêpe and garnish with parsley sprigs, if desired.

Soba Noodles with Peanut Sauce and Spinach

1 pound spinach
Large orange
1 egg
½ cup creamy peanut butter
¼ cup Japanese soy sauce
¼ cup mirin or sweet cooking wine
1 tablespoon honey
1 tablespoon rice vinegar or apple cider vinegar
1 teaspoon Worcestershire sauce
1 teaspoon spicy prepared mustard
½ pound soba noodles or good-quality spaghetti

1. Fill large stockpot with water to within 3 inches of top and bring to a boil over high heat.

2. Meanwhile, wash spinach in several changes of tepid water and remove tough stems. Halve orange and squeeze enough juice to measure ¼ cup. Separate egg, placing yolk in small bowl and reserving white for another use.

3. Place peanut butter, soy sauce, and mirin in container of food processor or blender and process until blended. Add honey, vinegar, Worcestershire sauce, and mustard, and process until blended. Add orange juice and process until blended. Add egg yolk and process until blended. Transfer sauce to small bowl, cover, and refrigerate until needed.

4. Plunge spinach into boiling water and blanch 1 minute, or until just wilted. Turn into colander and refresh under cold running water. Squeeze spinach dry, turn onto work surface, and press into 2-inch roll about 8 inches long. Cut roll into ½-inch-thick slices; set aside.

5. Bring 2 quarts water to a boil in large stockpot over high heat.

6. Cook noodles in boiling water 5 to 6 minutes, or if using spaghetti, according to package directions, until *al dente*. Turn noodles into colander and refresh under cold running water about 5 minutes, or until thoroughly chilled. Set aside to drain well.

7. To serve, divide noodles among 4 dinner plates. Top with peanut sauce and spinach rounds.

ADDED TOUCH

In Japan, foods that are batter-dipped and then deep-fried are called *tempura*. Here you fry pieces of fruit and, surprisingly, balls of ice cream. *Tempura* flour, used in the batter, is a low-gluten wheat flour available at Oriental markets. If you like, serve the *tempura* with honey, cinnamon sugar, or chocolate sauce for dipping.

Fruit and Ice Cream Tempura

1⅓ cups tempura flour or all-purpose flour
Large egg
Large apple, such as Delicious or McIntosh
Large pear
Medium-size banana
4 slices soft white bread
3 cups vegetable oil
½ pint vanilla ice cream

1. Place flour, 1 cup ice water, and egg in medium-size bowl and stir just until blended. Refrigerate batter 1 hour.

2. Peel, halve, and core apple and pear. Cut each fruit into 8 wedges. Peel banana and cut crosswise into 4 pieces.

3. Trim crusts from bread and, using rolling pin, roll bread very thin. Cut each slice diagonally into 2 triangles.

4. Heat oil in deep fryer over medium-high heat until deep-fat thermometer registers 350 degrees.

5. While oil is heating, remove ice cream from freezer. Place a rounded tablespoon of ice cream on each bread triangle and wrap bread completely around ice cream. Place each ice cream ball in freezer as it is formed.

6. Line plate with double thickness of paper towels. Dip 5 or 6 pieces of fruit in batter and fry in oil 1½ minutes. Transfer with tongs to paper-towel-lined plate. Fry remaining fruit in same manner.

7. Transfer fruit tempura to serving platter. Increase oil temperature to 375 degrees.

8. Quickly dip ice cream balls in batter and fry in oil 30 to 45 seconds. Using slotted spoon, transfer to serving platter with fruit tempura and serve immediately.

Broiled Eggplant with Miso Sauce
Pan-Fried Tofu with Vegetables
Sweet and Sour Rice

Eggplant with miso sauce and sweet and sour rice accompany golden cubes of fried tofu with vegetables.

The broiled eggplant halves are served with a sauce based on *miso* paste. *Miso* is a seasoning and soup base produced from fermented soy paste and yeast. This versatile high-protein product has a consistency ranging from smooth and soft to firm and chunky, and its color varies from white to dark brown; the deeper the color, the more pronounced the flavor. There is no equivalent for its unique taste. *Miso* is sold in Oriental markets and health food stores. Refrigerate it and use it within three months. Another ingredient in the sauce is Oriental sesame oil. This highly aromatic oil, made from toasted sesame seeds, is for seasoning, not cooking. Buy a Japanese or Chinese brand and store it in a cool, dark place.

To fry the tofu successfully, drain it well to remove all excess water and to firm it. Rolling the tofu in cornstarch keeps it from crumbling during frying.

WHAT TO DRINK

A Japanese beer suits this menu. Or, try a Riesling from California or the Pacific Northwest.

SHOPPING LIST AND STAPLES

4 Japanese or baby eggplants (about 1 pound total weight)

Small bunch broccoli (about ½ pound)
Small head cauliflower (about ½ pound)
Small head Chinese cabbage (about ½ pound)
2 ounces snow peas
Jumbo egg
3 cakes tofu (about 1½ pounds total weight)
4-ounce can sliced bamboo shoots
6 tablespoons vegetable oil
⅔ cup Oriental sesame oil, approximately
3 tablespoons rice vinegar or apple cider vinegar
½ cup Japanese soy sauce
¼ cup plus 2 tablespoons honey (optional)
1½ tablespoons Worcestershire sauce
¼ cup miso paste
2 cups Japanese sweet rice
2 tablespoons sesame seeds
¼ cup sugar, approximately, or ⅔ cup if not using honey
½ cup plus 2 tablespoons cornstarch
½ cup mirin or sweet cooking wine, approximately

UTENSILS

Large stockpot
Large heavy-gauge skillet
12-inch skillet
3 medium-size saucepans, 1 heavy-gauge with cover
2 small saucepans, 1 nonaluminum
Small baking pan
Large nonaluminum bowl
2 small bowls
Large colander with saucepan cover to fit
Strainer
Measuring cups and spoons
Chef's knife
Paring knife
Slotted spatula
Metal tongs
Pastry brush

START-TO-FINISH STEPS

1. Follow tofu recipe steps 1 and 2, rice recipe steps 1 and 2, and eggplant recipe steps 1 through 4.
2. Follow rice recipe step 3 and tofu recipe steps 3 and 4.
3. Follow rice recipe step 4 and eggplant recipe step 5.
4. Follow rice recipe step 5 and tofu recipe steps 5 through 8.
5. Follow rice recipe steps 6 through 12 and tofu recipe steps 9 and 10.
6. Follow eggplant recipe step 6 and rice recipe step 13.
7. Follow tofu recipe step 11, eggplant recipe step 7, and serve with rice.

RECIPES

Broiled Eggplant with Miso Sauce

4 Japanese or baby eggplants (about 1 pound total weight)

2 tablespoons sesame seeds
¼ cup miso paste
Jumbo egg
¼ cup mirin or sweet cooking wine
6 tablespoons sugar or honey
2 tablespoons Oriental sesame oil
¼ cup vegetable oil

1. Preheat oven to 350 degrees. Wash eggplants and dry with paper towels. Trim stem ends and halve each eggplant lengthwise. Using sharp paring knife, make 3 diagonal slits on skin side and cut side of each half.
2. Spread sesame seeds in small baking pan and toast in oven, shaking pan occasionally, 5 minutes.
3. Meanwhile, combine miso paste and egg in small saucepan and stir until smooth. Add mirin, sugar or honey, and sesame oil, and stir well. Set aside.
4. Remove sesame seeds from oven and add to miso mixture. Stir until combined and set aside.
5. Heat vegetable oil in 12-inch skillet over medium-high heat until hot. Add eggplant halves and cook, turning occasionally with tongs, 3 to 4 minutes, or until slightly charred on both sides. Divide eggplant halves among 4 small plates. Set aside until ready to serve.
6. Just before serving, heat miso mixture in saucepan over low heat, stirring constantly, just until it comes to a boil.
7. Using pastry brush, spread eggplants with miso mixture.

Pan-Fried Tofu with Vegetables

3 cakes tofu (about 1½ pounds total weight)
Small bunch broccoli (about ½ pound)
Small head cauliflower (about ½ pound)
Small head Chinese cabbage (about ½ pound)
6 tablespoons Japanese soy sauce
6 tablespoons Oriental sesame oil
3 tablespoons mirin or sweet cooking wine
2½ tablespoons sugar
1½ tablespoons Worcestershire sauce
½ cup plus 2 tablespoons cornstarch
2 tablespoons vegetable oil

1. Wrap tofu in clean kitchen towel or several thicknesses of paper towels and cover with heavy plate to press out excess moisture. Allow tofu to stand this way about 20 minutes.

Chinese cabbage

2. Meanwhile, wash broccoli, cauliflower, and cabbage, and dry with paper towels. Break broccoli and cauliflower heads into bite-size florets. You should have 2½ to 3 cups each. Remove cabbage leaves from stalks and halve lengthwise. Set aside.

3. Combine 1 cup water, soy sauce, sesame oil, mirin, sugar, and Worcestershire sauce in medium-size saucepan; set aside.

4. Dissolve 2 tablespoons cornstarch in ¼ cup water in small bowl; set aside.

5. Fill large stockpot half full with water and bring to a boil over high heat.

6. Spread remaining ½ cup cornstarch on plate. Cut each tofu cake into quarters and dredge each piece lightly in cornstarch.

7. Heat vegetable oil in large heavy-gauge skillet over medium heat until hot.

8. Line platter with paper towels. Add tofu to skillet and fry 5 minutes on each side, or until golden brown. Using slotted spatula, transfer tofu to paper-towel-lined platter to drain.

9. Add cauliflower to boiling water and cook 1 minute. Add broccoli to pot with cauliflower and cook 1 minute. Add cabbage to pot and cook 30 seconds, or until cabbage is wilted. Turn all vegetables into colander to drain. Cover colander to keep vegetables warm.

10. Place saucepan of soy sauce mixture over medium-high heat and bring mixture to a boil. Gradually stir in cornstarch mixture and cook, stirring constantly, about 3 minutes, or until sauce is dark brown and syrupy. Remove pan from heat.

11. Divide tofu among 4 dinner plates and surround with vegetables. Stir sauce, pour over tofu, and serve.

Sweet and Sour Rice

2 ounces snow peas
4-ounce can sliced bamboo shoots
2 cups Japanese sweet rice
2 tablespoons Japanese soy sauce
1½ teaspoons Oriental sesame oil
2 tablespoons sugar
3 tablespoons rice vinegar or apple cider vinegar

1. Wash, dry, trim, and string snow peas. Drain bamboo shoots in colander and set aside ¾ cup.

2. Place rice in medium-size heavy-gauge saucepan. Rinse rice in cold water, drain, and repeat 3 or 4 times to remove surface starch. (Water will be milky in color at first and after several rinses will become almost clear.) Turn rice into strainer to drain, then return rice to pan and add 2 cups water. Set aside for about 10 minutes.

3. Cook rice, covered, over high heat 5 minutes, or until it begins to steam.

4. Reduce heat to medium-low and cook rice another 7 minutes.

5. Reduce heat to low and cook rice another 13 minutes.

6. Remove pan from heat and let rice stand, covered, 15 minutes.

7. Meanwhile, fill medium-size saucepan half-full of water and bring to a boil over high heat.

8. Place soy sauce, sesame oil, and 1 tablespoon sugar in small bowl and stir to combine. Add bamboo shoots and set aside to marinate.

9. Add snow peas to boiling water and cook 3 minutes. Turn into colander to drain.

10. Heat vinegar and remaining 1 tablespoon sugar in small nonaluminum saucepan over medium heat 2 to 3 minutes, or until sugar is dissolved. Do not allow mixture to boil.

11. Meanwhile, transfer rice to large nonaluminum bowl.

12. Add vinegar mixture to rice. Drain bamboo shoots in strainer and add to rice. Add snow peas and toss to combine all ingredients.

13. Divide rice among 4 small bowls.

ADDED TOUCH

These sweet-potato balls, call *kinton* in Japan, have chestnuts hidden in their centers. Imported French canned chestnuts (*marrons*) are costly, so you may prefer to use the less expensive Asian variety, which is perfectly satisfactory for this recipe. Serve the dessert with steaming cups of Japanese green tea.

Sweet Potato-Chestnut Balls

3 eggs
1¼ pounds sweet potatoes
½ cup sugar
⅛ teaspoon salt
10-ounce can sweetened or water-packed chestnuts

1. Separate eggs, placing yolks in small bowl and reserving whites for another use.

2. Peel sweet potatoes and cut into 1-inch pieces. Place potatoes in large bowl of cold water to soak 30 minutes to 1 hour.

3. Bring large saucepan of water to a boil over high heat. Drain sweet potatoes in colander.

4. Add sweet potatoes to boiling water and cook 15 minutes, or until tender.

5. While sweet potatoes are cooking, combine sugar and ¾ cup water in small saucepan and bring to a boil over medium heat. Boil syrup 3 minutes. Remove pan from heat.

6. When cooked, drain sweet potatoes in colander, place in large bowl, and mash.

7. Turn mashed potatoes into medium-size saucepan. Gradually stir in sugar syrup and cook, stirring, over medium heat 1 minute. Add egg yolks and salt, and stir to combine well. Cook mixture, stirring constantly, 10 minutes, or until quite dry. Remove pan from heat and allow potato mixture to cool. Drain chestnuts in strainer.

8. When cool, place a heaping tablespoon of sweet potato mixture on a damp kitchen towel. Press a chestnut into center and form potato mixture into a ball around it. Repeat with remaining sweet potato mixture and chestnuts. Place balls on plate and cover with plastic wrap. Let stand at room temperature or refrigerate until ready to serve.

Julie Sahni

J ulie Sahni feels that eating meatless meals—at least some of the time—"improves your palate and prolongs your life." Like all good Indian cooks, she knows how to combine seasonings artfully to give each dish a distinctive character: She uses some herbs and spices for aroma, some for color, some for piquancy, and others as binders and thickeners. Her aim, whether she is teaching a class or cooking for family and friends, is to erase the Western idea that all Indian dishes are curries.

As you will discover in this collection of recipes, Indian spices can transform what might otherwise have been mundane dishes of vegetables or grains. In Menu 1, the vegetables for the stew cook in a yogurt sauce flavored with ginger, chilies, curry powder, cumin, mustard seeds, and coriander. As a foil for this spicy dish, Julie Sahni offers a platter of aromatic *basmati* rice garnished with tomatoes and cashews. Dessert is a slightly sweetened confection of sour cream, yogurt, and cream cheese.

In her second menu, the cook uses nine different spices to produce a fragrant and colorful vegetable pilaf. As side dishes, she offers braised tomatoes with chilies in a garlic sauce, and a cooling herbed yogurt salad.

Menu 3 proves that even a few spices judiciously used can make a dish savory. The meal features fresh homemade Indian cheese flavored with scallions, coriander, and black pepper, and fried eggplant slices sprinkled with cumin and Cayenne. A simple rice pilaf with raisins and sunflower seeds completes the meal.

For a dramatic presentation, serve the curried vegetable stew from a Dutch oven and encircle the basmati *rice with tomatoes and cashews. Cream pudding garnished with pistachio slices is the dessert.*

Madras Vegetable Stew
Basmati Rice
Indian Cream Pudding

In preparing the vegetable stew, you will learn a typical Indian cooking technique: frying spices in hot fat to release their flavor before combining them with other ingredients. Here, the spices are curry powder and whole cumin and mustard seeds. The trick is to shake the pan constantly during frying to prevent burning and to watch carefully because the spices brown very quickly.

Rice is an integral part of most Indian meals, and *basmati*, grown in the foothills of the Himalayas, is particularly aromatic and delicious. *Basmati* has a long slender grain and a characteristic nutty fragrance. It can be purchased in Indian groceries and specialty food shops, or see page 103 for mail-order sources. Although cooking *basmati* is not particularly difficult, remember that the rice should be picked over for tiny sticks or pebbles, and it must be washed and soaked in cold water before cooking. Washing removes any bran, husks, or other light debris as well as excess starch; soaking softens the grains so they do not crack during cooking.

WHAT TO DRINK

Cold beer or ale would suit this meal, as would a well-chilled, crisp white wine such as a French Muscadet or an Italian Verdicchio.

SHOPPING LIST AND STAPLES

Medium-size bunch broccoli (about 1 pound)
¾ pound yellow summer squash, butternut squash, or pumpkin
2 ripe plum tomatoes (about ½ pound total weight)
4 fresh hot green chilies
Medium-size red onion
1-inch piece fresh ginger
Small bunch coriander
½ pint sour cream
1 pint plain yogurt
8-ounce package cream cheese
¼ cup plus 1 tablespoon light vegetable oil
1-pound package basmati rice
½ cup confectioners' sugar
1½ teaspoons cornstarch
⅓ cup whole roasted cashews
1 tablespoon unsalted raw pistachios
2 teaspoons curry powder
1½ teaspoons ground cumin

1 teaspoon mustard seeds
½ teaspoon cumin seeds
¼ teaspoon freshly grated nutmeg
¼ teaspoon saffron threads
Salt
Freshly ground pepper

UTENSILS

Food processor or blender
Medium-size skillet with cover
Dutch oven or large heavy-gauge saucepan, with cover
3-quart saucepan
Large bowl
Small bowl
Fine strainer or colander
Measuring cups and spoons
Chef's knife
Paring knife
Wooden spoon
Thin rubber gloves

START-TO-FINISH STEPS

Thirty minutes ahead: Set out cream cheese to come to room temperature for pudding recipe.

1. Follow rice recipe step 1 and pudding recipe steps 1 through 3.
2. Follow stew recipe steps 1 through 3 and rice recipe step 2.
3. Follow stew recipe steps 4 and 5 and rice recipe step 3.
4. Follow stew recipe step 6 and rice recipe step 4.
5. While rice is cooking, follow stew recipe step 7.
6. Follow rice recipe steps 5 and 6, stew recipe step 8, and serve.
7. Serve pudding for dessert.

RECIPES

Madras Vegetable Stew

Medium-size red onion
Medium-size bunch broccoli (about 1 pound)
¾ pound yellow summer squash, butternut squash, or pumpkin
1-inch piece fresh ginger
Small bunch coriander

4 fresh hot green chilies
1 cup plain yogurt
1½ teaspoons ground cumin
1½ teaspoons cornstarch
5 tablespoons light vegetable oil
2 teaspoons curry powder
Salt
½ teaspoon cumin seeds
1 teaspoon mustard seeds

1. Peel and halve onion. Cut each half into ¼-inch-thick slices. Set aside.
2. Wash broccoli and dry with paper towels. Trim stems and cut broccoli into 2-inch florets. Wash and trim summer squash, if using, and cut enough into ½-inch-thick slices to measure about 4 cups. If using butternut squash or pumpkin, halve, peel, seed, and cut enough into ¼-inch-thick slices to measure about 4 cups. Peel ginger and chop roughly. Wash coriander and pat dry. Remove enough coriander leaves and tender stems to measure ¼ cup loosely packed. Wearing rubber gloves, wash, stem, and split chilies.
3. Place ginger, coriander, chilies, yogurt, ground cumin, and cornstarch in blender or food processor and process until combined; set aside.
4. Heat 2 tablespoons oil in Dutch oven or large heavy-gauge saucepan over medium-high heat. When oil is hot, add curry powder and let sizzle, shaking pan constantly, about 10 seconds, or until fragrant. Add broccoli and squash and toss to coat with spices. Cook 1 minute. Add yogurt sauce, stir to combine, and season with salt to taste. Pour 1 cup water into blender or food processor container, shake to rinse, and pour water over vegetables; stir to combine.
5. Increase heat to high and bring mixture to a boil. Reduce heat to medium-low and cook, covered, 5 minutes.
6. Uncover pan, increase heat to high, and boil rapidly 1 minute; turn off heat.
7. Heat remaining 3 tablespoons oil in medium-size skillet over high heat. When oil is hot, add cumin seeds and mustard seeds. Keep cover of pan handy as seeds will sputter and pop. Shaking pan, cook seeds 1 to 2 minutes, or until cumin turns dark and sputtering subsides. Add onion, and toss and stir quickly about 2 minutes, or until onion begins to color. Turn off heat.
8. To serve, transfer stew to large serving dish and top with onion mixture.

Basmati Rice

1 cup basmati rice
2 ripe plum tomatoes (about ½ pound total weight)
⅓ cup whole roasted cashews
Salt
Freshly ground pepper

1. Place rice in large bowl and wash in several changes of cold water until water runs clear. Add enough water to cover rice by at least 1 inch and let soak 30 minutes.

2. Bring 2 quarts water to a boil in 3-quart saucepan over high heat.
3. Wash and core tomatoes; thinly slice tomatoes and set aside.
4. Drain rice and add to boiling water. Gently stir to prevent rice from settling to bottom of pan. When water returns to a boil, cook rice, uncovered, 4½ to 5 minutes, or until tender.
5. Immediately pour cooked rice into fine strainer or colander and drain.
6. Spoon rice onto serving platter and surround with tomato slices and cashews. Sprinkle tomatoes with salt and pepper to taste and serve.

Indian Cream Pudding

1 cup sour cream
⅓ cup plain yogurt
½ cup cream cheese, at room temperature
½ cup confectioners' sugar
¼ teaspoon saffron threads
¼ teaspoon freshly grated nutmeg
1 tablespoon unsalted raw pistachios

1. Combine sour cream, yogurt, cream cheese, and sugar in small bowl.
2. Lightly crush saffron with fingers and add to mixture in bowl. Add nutmeg and stir until mixture is thoroughly blended and smooth. Spoon pudding into 4 stemmed glasses or dessert bowls.
3. Slice pistachios lengthwise and sprinkle equally over puddings. Cover glasses or bowls and refrigerate until ready to serve.

━━━━━━━
ADDED TOUCH

A vegetable-fruit relish is a frequent part of Indian meals. This one is simple and quick to make and can be prepared just before mealtime. Serve it in place of a salad. Leftovers can be refrigerated in a tightly covered container for up to four days.

Carrot and Mango Relish

Medium-size carrot
Small unripe mango (about ¼ pound)
½ teaspoon Cayenne pepper
1¼ teaspoons salt
½ teaspoon dry mustard
2 tablespoons light vegetable oil

1. Peel and trim carrot and halve lengthwise. Cut each half crosswise into ⅛-inch-thick slices and place in small bowl. Peel and pit mango and cut flesh into ⅛-inch-thick slices; add to carrots. Add Cayenne, salt, and mustard and toss to mix well.
2. Heat oil in small skillet until smoking. Pour hot oil over vegetables and immediately stir to combine. Set relish aside, uncovered, at room temperature until ready to serve.

Fragrant Vegetable Pilaf
Braised Tomatoes with Chilies in Garlic Sauce
Zucchini Raita

The highly seasoned vegetable pilaf garnished with nuts and black grapes is delicious with braised tomatoes and refreshing raita.

Rice pilaf in its most basic form is simply rice that has been sautéed in fat, then simmered in liquid. The fat keeps the grains separated, and the gentle simmering makes them tender. An Indian pilaf often includes a number of ingredients besides rice: This recipe has vegetables, yogurt, and spices. Traditionally, the whole cinnamon stick and bay leaves are left in when the rice is served on a platter, but only for their decorative appearance. They are not meant to be eaten. The optional garnish of black grapes and almonds also provides a visual highlight—and an unusual flavor contrast as well.

This version of the yogurt salad called *raita* in India is made by stirring spices and barely cooked zucchini into a yogurt-sour cream mixture. Indian cooks would use a rich homemade buffalo-milk yogurt, but a good-quality commercial whole-milk yogurt makes a satisfactory substitute here.

WHAT TO DRINK

The assertive flavors and aromas of these dishes require a medium-bodied dry white wine. A California Sauvignon Blanc or a California or Alsatian Gewürztraminer would be a good choice.

SHOPPING LIST AND STAPLES

1½ pounds ripe tomatoes, preferably
  Italian plum
Small head cauliflower (about 1 pound)
½ pound fresh peas, or 10 ounce-package frozen
Medium-size carrot
Small zucchini
4 fresh hot green chilies
Small bunch scallions
Large onion
8 large cloves garlic
1-inch piece fresh ginger
Small bunch mint
Small bunch coriander
Small bunch black Emperor grapes (optional)
½ pint sour cream
1 pint plain yogurt
¾ cup light vegetable oil, approximately
1 cup long-grain white rice
1½ teaspoons sugar
⅓ cup toasted slivered almonds (optional)
2 whole dried red pepper pods
1¾ teaspoons ground cumin
1 teaspoon mustard seeds
1 teaspoon cumin seeds
1 teaspoon ground coriander
½ teaspoon turmeric
½ teaspoon Cayenne pepper or red pepper
  flakes, approximately
3-inch stick cinnamon
9 whole cloves
2 bay leaves
Salt

UTENSILS

Large heavy-gauge sauté pan with cover
Medium-size heavy-gauge sauté pan
  with cover
Small skillet
Medium-size bowl
Small bowl
Colander
Measuring cups and spoons
Chef's knife
Paring knife

2 wooden spoons
Metal spatula
Grater
Vegetable peeler (optional)
Thin rubber gloves

START-TO-FINISH STEPS

1. Peel ginger. Cut two ⅛-inch-thick slices for raita recipe. Finely chop enough remaining ginger to measure 1 tablespoon for pilaf recipe.
2. Follow pilaf recipe steps 1 through 6.
3. While pilaf is cooking, follow tomatoes recipe steps 1 and 2.
4. While tomatoes are cooking, follow raita recipe steps 1 and 2 and pilaf recipe step 7.
5. While pilaf continues to cook, follow raita recipe steps 3 and 4 and tomatoes recipe step 3.
6. Follow pilaf recipe steps 8 and 9.
7. Follow raita recipe step 5, tomatoes recipe step 4, pilaf recipe step 10, and serve.

RECIPES

Fragrant Vegetable Pilaf

Small head cauliflower (about 1 pound)
Medium-size carrot
Large onion
½ pound fresh peas, or ½ cup frozen
¼ cup plus 2 tablespoons light vegetable oil
1 teaspoon cumin seeds
3-inch stick cinnamon
9 whole cloves
2 bay leaves
1 tablespoon finely chopped fresh ginger
1 teaspoon ground cumin
1 teaspoon ground coriander
½ teaspoon turmeric
¼ to ½ teaspoon Cayenne pepper or red pepper flakes
1½ teaspoons salt
½ cup plain yogurt
1 cup long-grain white rice
Small bunch black Emperor grapes (optional)
⅓ cup toasted slivered almonds (optional)

1. Wash cauliflower and dry with paper towels. Trim cauliflower and cut enough into 2- to 2½-inch florets to measure about 4 cups. Peel and trim carrot and cut cross-wise into ¼-inch-thick slices. Peel onion and finely chop enough to measure ½ cup. If using fresh peas, shell enough to measure ½ cup.

2. Heat oil in large heavy-gauge sauté pan over high heat 2 minutes.

3. Meanwhile, combine cumin seeds, cinnamon stick, cloves, and bay leaves in small bowl. When oil is hot, add spices and, shaking pan constantly, let spices sizzle about 30 seconds, or until fragrant. Add onion and ginger and cook, stirring, about 4 minutes, or until onion is lightly colored.

4. Reduce heat to medium. Add ground cumin, coriander, turmeric, Cayenne, and salt to pan and continue to cook, stirring, 1 minute. Add cauliflower and carrot and toss to coat well with spices.

5. Increase heat to high. Add yogurt, stir until well combined, and cook 2 minutes. Add rice, stir, and cook 30 seconds. Add 2 cups water, and allow mixture to come to a boil.

6. When mixture boils, reduce heat to medium and cook, partially covered, 10 minutes.

7. Add peas and stir gently. Cover pan tightly, reduce heat to very low, and cook 8 to 10 minutes, or until rice is soft and vegetables are tender.

8. Turn off heat and let pilaf rest, covered, 10 minutes.

9. Meanwhile, wash and dry grapes, if using, and remove from stems.

10. Fluff pilaf with fork, remove bay leaves and cinnamon stick, and divide pilaf among 4 dinner plates. Garnish with grapes and toasted almonds, if desired.

Braised Tomatoes with Chilies in Garlic Sauce

1½ pounds ripe tomatoes, preferably Italian plum
8 large cloves garlic
4 fresh hot green chilies
3 tablespoons light vegetable oil
1 teaspoon mustard seeds
2 whole dried red pepper pods
1 teaspoon salt

1. Wash, dry, and core tomatoes. If using plum tomatoes, quarter lengthwise; if using round tomatoes, cut into 1-inch wedges. Peel garlic and cut each clove lengthwise into 2 or 3 slices. Wearing rubber gloves, slit chilies lengthwise; remove seeds and trim stem ends.

2. Heat oil in medium-size heavy-gauge sauté pan over high heat. When oil is hot, add mustard seeds and dried pepper pods. Keep cover of pan handy as pepper seeds will sputter and pop. Shaking pan, cook seeds and pods until sputtering stops and pods turn dark. Add garlic, chilies, and salt, and sauté 1 minute. Add tomatoes and stir carefully to coat evenly with spices (tomato pieces should remain as intact as possible). Bring mixture to a simmer, reduce heat to medium-low, and cook, partially covered, 20 minutes, without stirring.

3. Remove pan from heat and let tomatoes stand, covered, until ready to serve.

4. To serve, using metal spatula divide tomatoes and sauce among 4 dinner plates.

Zucchini Raita

Small zucchini
2 large scallions
Two ⅛-inch-thick slices fresh ginger
Small bunch mint
Small bunch coriander
1⅓ cups plain yogurt
⅓ cup sour cream
1½ teaspoons sugar
¾ teaspoon salt
2 tablespoons light vegetable oil
¾ teaspoon ground cumin

1. Wash zucchini and dry with paper towels; trim ends. Using coarse side of grater, grate zucchini into colander. Press and squeeze zucchini firmly to remove excess moisture. Blot with paper towels and set aside in colander.

2. Wash, dry, and trim scallions, discarding dark green tops. Cut white parts of scallions crosswise into ⅛-inch-thick slices. You should have about ¼ cup. Finely dice ginger. Wash and dry mint and coriander. Reserve 4 sprigs mint for garnish and finely chop enough remaining mint and coriander leaves to measure ⅓ cup each.

3. In medium-size bowl, combine yogurt, sour cream, sugar, and salt. Add scallions, ginger, and chopped mint and coriander, and mix well.

4. Heat oil in small skillet over high heat until very hot. Turn off heat, sprinkle oil with ground cumin, and immediately add zucchini. Toss zucchini in hot oil until barely cooked. Add zucchini to yogurt mixture and blend well. Set aside until ready to serve.

5. To serve, divide raita among 4 dinner plates and garnish with reserved mint sprigs.

Fresh Indian Cheese with Bell Peppers
Spiced Eggplant with Mango Chutney
Pilaf

Molded homemade Indian cheese with coriander and peppers can be served with or before the fried eggplant and pilaf.

resh homemade cheese, a principal source of protein for Indian vegetarians, resembles a dry ricotta or pot cheese. To make the cheese successfully, be sure the milk is at a rolling boil before you add the lemon juice. The curds should begin to surface within seconds. Sometimes the curds form before all the lemon juice is added. If this happens, do not add the remaining lemon juice. If, on the other hand, the curds do not form after all the juice has been added, add a bit more juice until the white solids separate from the whey. Indian cheese can be made using vinegar or yogurt as a starter, but the cook prefers lemon juice because it creates a more delicate cheese. You can prepare the cheese up to five days in advance and refrigerate it in a covered container.

WHAT TO DRINK

Either a light red wine or a fairly full-bodied white would be enjoyable with this menu. For red, try a French Beaujolais or a California Gamay Beaujolais. For white, choose a California Chardonnay or a French white Burgundy such as a Mâcon or a Saint-Véran.

SHOPPING LIST AND STAPLES

Medium-size eggplant (1 to 1¼ pounds)
Small bunch red radishes with leaves attached (optional)
Medium-size green bell pepper
Medium-size red bell pepper
Medium-size yellow bell pepper
4 fresh hot green chilies (optional)
Small bunch scallions
Small bunch coriander
4 large lemons
3 quarts milk
2 tablespoons unsalted butter
4-ounce jar mango chutney
½ cup plus 1 tablespoon light vegetable oil, approximately
2 tablespoons all-purpose flour, approximately
¾ cup long-grain white rice
2 tablespoons roasted sunflower seeds
¼ cup dark raisins
1½ teaspoons ground cumin
1 teaspoon ground coriander
½ teaspoon Cayenne pepper
½ teaspoon fennel seeds
Salt
Freshly ground black pepper

UTENSILS

2 large heavy-gauge skillets
Medium-size skillet
Large deep heavy-gauge nonaluminum saucepan
Medium-size saucepan with cover
Four 4-ounce custard cups, or teacups
Large bowl
Medium-size bowl
Small bowl
Colander
Measuring cups and spoons
Chef's knife
Paring knife
2 wooden spoons
Metal spatula
Citrus juicer (optional)
Cheesecloth
Thin rubber gloves (optional)

START-TO-FINISH STEPS

1. Follow cheese recipe steps 1 through 6.
2. While cheese is draining, follow eggplant recipe step 1.
3. Follow cheese recipe steps 7 and 8 and pilaf recipe steps 1 and 2.
4. While rice is cooking, follow cheese recipe step 9.
5. Follow pilaf recipe step 3.
6. While rice continues to cook, follow eggplant recipe steps 2 through 4.
7. Follow pilaf recipe step 4.
8. While pilaf rests, follow cheese recipe steps 10 and 11 and eggplant recipe step 5.
9. Follow pilaf recipe step 5, eggplant recipe step 6, and serve with cheese.

RECIPES

Fresh Indian Cheese with Bell Peppers

4 large lemons
3 quarts milk
1 teaspoon salt, approximately
Medium-size green bell pepper
Medium-size red bell pepper
Medium-size yellow bell pepper
2 scallions
Small bunch coriander
1 tablespoon light vegetable oil
1 teaspoon ground coriander
¼ teaspoon freshly ground black pepper
4 fresh hot green chilies for garnish (optional)

1. Halve 3 lemons and squeeze enough juice into small bowl to measure ¾ cup; set aside. Reserve remaining lemon for garnish.
2. Place milk and 1 teaspoon salt in large deep heavy-gauge nonaluminum saucepan over high heat. Cook, stirring occasionally to prevent sticking, 12 to 15 minutes, or until milk is just below the boiling point.
3. Meanwhile, wash and dry bell peppers. Core and halve peppers and cut lengthwise into ½-inch-wide strips; set aside. (See illustration.)
4. Wash and trim scallions; discard dark green tops. Cut white parts of scallions crosswise into ⅛-inch-thick slices and place in medium-size bowl. Wash and dry coriander; set aside 4 large sprigs for garnish. Remove enough re-

maining coriander leaves from tough stems to measure ¼ cup loosely packed. Coarsely chop coriander leaves and add to scallions.

Coriander

5. Line colander with double thickness of dampened cheesecloth.

6. When milk comes to a rolling boil, add lemon juice and stir gently. Almost immediately, milk will curdle and milky white curd will float to surface; liquid whey will turn greenish yellow. Turn mixture into colander to drain 5 minutes.

7. When whey has drained off, pour 2 cups cold water over cheese and drain about 30 seconds. Gather together corners of cheesecloth and squeeze cheese gently to remove as much water as possible. Return cheese, still wrapped in cheesecloth, to colander and place in sink. Weight cheese with 1-pound can and let drain 10 to 15 minutes.

8. Meanwhile, heat dry medium-size skillet over high heat 2 minutes. Add vegetable oil and ground coriander; immediately add bell pepper strips. Sprinkle with salt to taste and toss peppers quickly to coat evenly with spices. Let peppers cook undisturbed 1 minute. Toss peppers again, reduce heat to very low, and cook another 2 minutes. Remove pan from heat and set aside.

9. Remove cheese from cheesecloth and add to bowl with scallions and coriander. Add black pepper and mix thoroughly with hands; cheese should be silky-soft without being pasty. Lightly oil four 4-ounce custard cups, or teacups. Pack cheese into cups and set aside until ready to serve.

10. If using chilies for garnish, wearing rubber gloves, wash, dry, stem, and seed chilies. Finely chop chilies; set aside. Wash and dry reserved lemon and cut into 8 slices for garnish.

11. To serve, run knife around edges of cups to loosen cheese and unmold onto 4 salad plates. Divide pepper slices among plates. Garnish each serving with a coriander sprig, 2 lemon slices, and finely chopped chilies if desired.

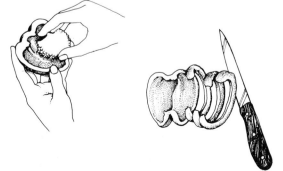

Core and slice bell peppers.

Spiced Eggplant with Mango Chutney

Medium-size eggplant (1 to 1¼ pounds)
1½ teaspoons ground cumin
½ teaspoon Cayenne pepper
¼ teaspoon freshly ground black pepper
2 tablespoons all-purpose flour, approximately
½ cup light vegetable oil, approximately
8 red radishes with leaves attached, for garnish
   (optional)
4-ounce jar mango chutney

1. Wash eggplant and dry with paper towels. Trim ends and cut eggplant crosswise into approximately ½-inch-thick slices, allowing 2 to 3 slices per person. Place eggplant in large bowl and sprinkle with cumin, Cayenne, and black pepper. Toss eggplant to coat evenly with spices; set aside.

2. Place 2 large heavy-gauge skillets over high heat.

3. While pans are heating, sprinkle about 2 tablespoons flour over eggplant slices and toss to coat evenly. If necessary, add more flour.

4. Pour about ¼ cup oil into each skillet, using just enough oil to form thin layer on bottom of pan. Divide eggplant slices between skillets, arranging them in a single layer in each. Fry slices about 4 minutes on each side, or until nicely browned on both sides, adding a bit more oil if necessary.

5. Wash radishes, if using, leaving leaves and root ends intact; set aside.

6. To serve, arrange eggplant slices on 4 dinner plates and spoon some chutney over each portion. Garnish each plate with 2 radishes, if desired.

Pilaf

2 tablespoons unsalted butter
½ teaspoon fennel seeds
¼ cup dark raisins
¾ cup long-grain white rice
Salt (optional)
2 tablespoons roasted sunflower seeds

1. Melt butter in medium-size saucepan over medium-high heat. Add fennel seeds and, shaking pan constantly, let seeds sizzle 30 seconds, or until fragrant. Add raisins and toss until well coated with butter. Add rice, and about ½ teaspoon salt if desired. Reduce heat to medium-low and fry rice 30 seconds, or until well coated with butter but not browned. Add 1½ cups water, stir, and bring to a boil over high heat.

2. Reduce heat to medium and cook rice, partially covered, 8 to 10 minutes, or until most of water is absorbed.

3. Stir rice, tightly cover pan, and reduce heat to very low. Cook rice another 10 minutes, or until tender and fluffy.

4. Remove pan from heat and let pilaf rest, covered, 5 minutes.

5. To serve, fluff pilaf with fork and divide among 4 dinner plates. Sprinkle with roasted sunflower seeds.

Robert Pucci

Robert Pucci says he enjoys cooking Italian food because it is wholesome. "Properly prepared, Italian food is low in fat and not overly rich or heavy," he notes. "Moreover, Italian cuisine abounds with meatless delights." He particularly likes the fact that Italian dishes rarely need elaborate garnishing because their many colorful ingredients are beautiful in themselves.

Menu 1 is well balanced in taste, texture, and color, as well as in nutrients. It offers a meatless version of lasagna, in which the noodles are layered with a mixture of ricotta and *béchamel* (white sauce) and a pesto made more interesting by the addition of spinach and several kinds of nuts. The salad of freshly grated carrots is presented on a bed of escarole.

Menu 2 is a protein-rich meal in which five kinds of cheese are used to fill manicotti. With the baked pasta the cook offers a mixed salad of radicchio and two types of lettuce to satisfy his love for "red and green on the table."

Striking reds and greens again predominate in Menu 3. Light spinach *gnocchi* (dumplings) are served with a hearty salad of red potatoes, red onion, cannellini, green beans, and cherry tomatoes. In Italy the *gnocchi* would be a first course, followed by the salad.

The unusual lasagna casserole filled with aromatic pesto sauce and topped with creamy béchamel *bakes while you prepare the grated carrot salad.*

Pesto Lasagna
Grated Carrot Salad

Pesto sauce gives the hearty main-course casserole a rich green color and zesty flavor. To make a pesto, cooks traditionally use a mortar and pestle to grind together fresh basil, garlic, pine nuts *(pignoli)*, and Parmesan cheese. Here you have the option of using either fresh basil or a mixture of dried basil and parsley, and, to save time, you purée the ingredients in a food processor or blender.

In addition to pine nuts, pecans or walnuts and blanched almonds are also used in this pesto. Most supermarkets sell blanched almonds (almonds with their brown skins removed). If they are unavailable, you can easily blanch almonds at home: Place the nuts in a bowl and cover them with boiling water. After five minutes, drain off the water and slip off the skins with your fingers.

WHAT TO DRINK

The robust pesto requires a red wine with both body and fruit. A Chianti Classico or a Gattinara would be good, as would a mature California Zinfandel.

SHOPPING LIST AND STAPLES

10 ounces fresh spinach
Small head escarole
1½ pounds medium-size carrots
3 large cloves garlic
Large bunch fresh basil, or medium-size bunch fresh parsley plus 1 tablespoon dried basil
2 large lemons
1½ cups milk
4 tablespoons unsalted butter
3 ounces Parmesan cheese
1 ounce Romano cheese
8-ounce container whole-milk ricotta cheese
2-ounce jar small capers (optional)
1 cup good-quality olive oil, preferably virgin, approximately
1 tablespoon vegetable oil
½ pound fresh or dried lasagna
3 tablespoons all-purpose flour
6 whole shelled pecans or walnuts
1 tablespoon blanched almonds
1 tablespoon pine nuts
Salt
Freshly ground white pepper

UTENSILS

Food processor or blender
Large stockpot with cover
Large heavy-gauge nonaluminum skillet
Large baking pan
11 x 7-inch glass baking dish
2 medium-size bowls, 1 nonaluminum
Small bowl
Colander
Salad spinner (optional)
Measuring cups and spoons
Chef's knife
Paring knife
2 wooden spoons
Rubber spatula
Grater (if not using food processor)
Citrus juicer (optional)
Whisk
Vegetable peeler (optional)

START-TO-FINISH STEPS

1. Using food processor or grater, grate enough Parmesan to measure ¾ cup and enough Romano to measure ¼ cup for lasagna recipe; set aside separately.
2. Follow lasagna recipe steps 1 through 10.
3. While lasagna is baking, follow salad recipe steps 1 through 4.
4. Follow lasagna recipe step 11 and serve with salad.

RECIPES

Pesto Lasagna

Pesto:
10 ounces fresh spinach
Large bunch fresh basil, or medium-size bunch fresh parsley plus 1 tablespoon dried basil
3 large cloves garlic
1 tablespoon pine nuts
1 tablespoon blanched almonds
6 whole shelled pecans or walnuts
⅓ cup good-quality olive oil, preferably virgin, approximately
½ teaspoon salt
½ teaspoon freshly ground white pepper
¼ cup grated Parmesan cheese

¼ cup grated Romano cheese

2 tablespoons salt
1 tablespoon vegetable oil
½ pound fresh or dried lasagna

Béchamel:
4 tablespoons unsalted butter
3 tablespoons all-purpose flour
1½ cups milk
¼ teaspoon salt
¼ teaspoon freshly ground white pepper
¾ cup whole-milk ricotta cheese

½ cup grated Parmesan cheese

1. Bring 4 quarts water to a boil in large covered stockpot.
2. Meanwhile, remove and discard tough stems from spinach. Wash spinach carefully in several changes of tepid water; dry thoroughly in salad spinner.
3. Wash and dry fresh basil, if using, and discard tough stems. Set aside enough leaves to measure 1 cup lightly packed. If using parsley, wash and pat dry. Remove enough leaves to measure ¾ cup lightly packed and combine with 1 tablespoon dried basil. Peel garlic.

Basil

4. For pesto, in food processor or blender, combine spinach, basil, or parsley and dried basil, and chop coarsely, turning machine on and off to process. With machine running, add garlic, pine nuts, almonds, and pecans or walnuts, and process until blended. Add olive oil, ½ teaspoon salt, and pepper, and process until smooth. Add Parmesan and Romano and process until smooth paste forms. If pesto seems too dry, add 1 additional tablespoon olive oil. Set pesto aside.
5. When water comes to a boil, add 2 tablespoons salt and 1 tablespoon vegetable oil. Add lasagna and cook 45 seconds if fresh, or according to package directions until *al dente*. Drain lasagna in colander. Fill large baking pan with cold water and place lasagna in pan to cool, separating noodles so they do not stick together. Arrange cooled lasagna in single layer on damp kitchen towel and set aside.

6. For béchamel, melt butter in large heavy-gauge non-aluminum skillet over medium heat. Whisk in flour and cook, stirring constantly, 2 minutes. Do not allow mixture to brown. Whisk in milk, salt, and pepper. Increase heat to medium-high and cook, stirring, about 3 minutes, or until mixture comes to a boil. Reduce heat to low and simmer, whisking occasionally, 5 minutes. Remove pan from heat. Reserve ¼ cup béchamel in small bowl.
7. In medium-size bowl, combine remaining béchamel with ricotta. Cover surface of sauce with plastic wrap to prevent skin from forming.
8. Preheat oven to 450 degrees.
9. Butter 11 x 7-inch glass baking dish. Arrange one third of lasagna in single layer on bottom of baking dish. Spread half of ricotta mixture over lasagna and top with half of pesto mixture. Sprinkle with 1 tablespoon Parmesan. Add another layer of lasagna and cover with remaining ricotta, remaining pesto, and 1 tablespoon Parmesan. Place remaining lasagna on top and spread with reserved ¼ cup béchamel. Sprinkle with remaining Parmesan.
10. Bake lasagna on center rack of oven 15 to 20 minutes, or until béchamel is golden and lasagna is heated through.
11. Remove lasagna from oven and let stand 5 to 10 minutes. Cut lasagna into 4 portions and serve.

Grated Carrot Salad

1½ pounds medium-size carrots
Small head escarole
2 large lemons
⅔ cup good-quality olive oil, preferably virgin
¼ teaspoon salt
¼ teaspoon freshly ground white pepper
2-ounce jar small capers (optional)

1. Peel and trim carrots. Coarsely grate carrots using grater or food processor; you should have 8 to 9 cups. Set aside.
2. Wash escarole, separating leaves. Remove tough stems and dry leaves in salad spinner or with paper towels.
3. Halve lemons and squeeze enough juice to measure ¼ cup. In medium-size nonaluminum bowl, combine lemon juice, olive oil, salt, and pepper; whisk until well combined. Drain 2 teaspoons capers, if using, and add to dressing.
4. Divide escarole leaves among 4 dinner plates. Add carrots to dressing and toss to coat evenly. Mound carrots on top of escarole.

Manicotti with Five Cheeses
Tossed Salad with Parmesan Vinaigrette

Sure to please the heartiest eaters: manicotti stuffed with a rich mixture of eggs and five Italian cheeses and sauced with a smooth blend of tomatoes and seasonings. A tossed salad provides complementary colors.

Y ou can prepare the pasta using cannelloni rather than dried manicotti shells. Buy freshly made cannelloni at a reputable Italian grocery, or make your own at home and freeze them, if desired. To make and freeze cannelloni, prepare any standard pasta recipe, roll out the dough as thinly as possible, and cut the dough into 5 by 4-inch rectangles. Place each rectangle between two sheets of waxed paper, wrap these in plastic, and freeze them for up to 2 weeks. To prevent cracking, thaw the pasta for a few minutes before pulling off the waxed paper, then cook the frozen pasta in boiling water as you would fresh pasta, remembering that since the dough is frozen, the water will return to the boil more slowly. Begin timing the cooking—1½ to 2 minutes—when the water returns to the boil. Drain the pasta and blot with kitchen towels. To fill the cannelloni, spoon 3 tablespoons of the cheese mixture onto the center of each rectangle and loosely fold the sides over the filling.

WHAT TO DRINK

You can serve either a red or white wine here, but it should be dry and somewhat fruity. Try an Italian Soave or Valpolicella, or a California Chenin Blanc or Gamay Beaujolais.

SHOPPING LIST AND STAPLES

Small head escarole
Small head radicchio
1 head Belgian endive
Small yellow onion
1 large and 1 small clove garlic
Small bunch parsley
3 large eggs
6 tablespoons unsalted butter
3½ ounces Parmesan cheese
1 ounce Romano cheese
½ pound mozzarella cheese
¼ pound Provolone cheese
8-ounce container ricotta cheese
28-ounce can Italian plum tomatoes
¼ cup plus 2 tablespoons good-quality olive oil, preferably virgin
1 tablespoon vegetable oil
1 tablespoon red wine vinegar
1 tablespoon raspberry or other flavored wine vinegar
8-ounce package dried manicotti shells

Salt
Freshly ground pepper

UTENSILS

Food processor or blender
Stockpot
Large heavy-gauge nonaluminum saucepan
13 x 9 x 2-inch nonaluminum baking dish
Salad bowl
Large bowl
Small nonaluminum bowl
Colander
Salad spinner (optional)
Measuring cups and spoons
Chef's knife
Paring knife
2 wooden spoons
Rubber spatula
Grater (if not using food processor)
Whisk
Garlic press (optional)

START-TO-FINISH STEPS

1. Using food processor or grater, finely shred mozzarella and Provolone for manicotti recipe. Grate enough Romano cheese to measure ¼ cup and enough Parmesan to measure ¾ cup for manicotti recipe. Grate enough remaining Parmesan to measure 1 tablespoon for salad recipe. Peel large garlic clove for manicotti recipe and small clove for salad recipe.
2. Follow manicotti recipe steps 1 through 12.
3. While manicotti is baking, follow salad recipe steps 1 through 4.
4. Follow manicotti recipe step 13 and serve.

RECIPES

Manicotti with Five Cheeses

Small yellow onion
Large clove garlic, peeled
Small bunch parsley
6 tablespoons unsalted butter
Salt
¾ teaspoon freshly ground pepper
28-ounce can Italian plum tomatoes
3 large eggs
8-ounce container ricotta cheese
¾ cup grated Parmesan cheese
¼ cup grated Romano cheese
½ pound mozzarella cheese, finely shredded
¼ pound Provolone cheese, finely shredded
1 tablespoon vegetable oil
8 to 10 dried manicotti shells

1. Halve, peel, and coarsely chop onion; set aside. Crush garlic under flat blade of chef's knife.

2. Wash parsley and dry with paper towels. Finely chop enough parsley to measure 2 tablespoons; set aside. Reserve remaining parsley for another use.
3. Melt butter in large heavy-gauge nonaluminum saucepan over medium heat. Add onion and garlic and sauté 1 minute. Add ½ teaspoon salt, ½ teaspoon pepper, and tomatoes with their juice, breaking up tomatoes with wooden spoon. Cook, stirring from time to time to prevent sticking, 25 to 30 minutes, or until sauce is thickened.
4. Meanwhile, bring 4 quarts water to a boil in stockpot.
5. Break eggs into large bowl and whisk until frothy. Add parsley, ¼ teaspoon salt, and ¼ teaspoon pepper, and whisk to combine.
6. Add ricotta to eggs and stir well. Add Parmesan, Romano, mozzarella, and Provolone, and stir until well combined. Cover and refrigerate until needed.
7. Preheat oven to 375 degrees.
8. When water boils, add 1 teaspoon salt, if desired, and vegetable oil. Carefully add manicotti shells and cook according to package directions until *al dente*.
9. Drain manicotti in colander and rinse well under cold running water. Place shells on clean kitchen towel. Cover with second towel and blot gently to absorb excess water.
10. When tomato sauce has thickened, transfer to food processor or blender and purée.
11. Spread 3 to 4 tablespoons sauce on bottom of 13 by 9 by 2-inch nonaluminum baking dish. Spoon about 3 tablespoons cheese filling into each manicotti shell and place filled shells in baking dish. Pour remaining tomato sauce over manicotti, spreading evenly with rubber spatula.
12. Bake manicotti 20 minutes, or until sauce is bubbling and manicotti are heated through.
13. Divide manicotti among 4 dinner plates and serve.

Tossed Salad with Parmesan Vinaigrette

Small clove garlic, peeled
Small head escarole
Small head radicchio
1 head Belgian endive
¼ cup plus 2 tablespoons good-quality olive oil,
    preferably virgin
1 tablespoon red wine vinegar
1 tablespoon raspberry or other flavored wine vinegar
Salt and freshly ground pepper
1 tablespoon grated Parmesan cheese

1. Crush garlic under flat blade of chef's knife and rub surface of salad bowl with garlic; discard garlic.
2. Separate escarole, radicchio, and endive leaves. Wash thoroughly and dry in salad spinner, or with paper towels. Tear escarole and radicchio into bite-size pieces. Cut endive crosswise into 1-inch pieces. Place in salad bowl.
3. Combine olive oil, vinegars, and salt and pepper to taste in small nonaluminum bowl, and whisk until well blended. Add 1 teaspoon grated Parmesan and whisk until dressing becomes creamy.
4. Pour dressing over salad and toss. Divide salad among 4 dinner plates and sprinkle with remaining Parmesan.

Spinach Gnocchi with Butter and Parmesan
Mixed Vegetable Salad

Delicate spinach gnocchi coated with butter and Parmesan cheese go well with a mixed vegetable salad.

Italians enjoy *gnocchi* made from a variety of ingredients including potatoes, pumpkin, semolina, and puff paste, but the traditional spinach-ricotta *gnocchi* are the most delicate of all because the ratio of flour to other ingredients is quite low. Spinach *gnocchi* are sometimes known as *malfatti* (or "badly made"), since their delicacy makes shaping them uniformly rather difficult. The amount of flour you add will depend on the humidity in the air, and on how well you have dried the spinach. If you add too much flour, the dumplings become too heavy; if you add too little flour, they will be sticky and hard to shape, and will disintegrate during boiling. Add only as much flour as needed to make the dough hold together.

You can make *gnocchi* ahead of time and freeze them uncooked. To do so, arrange the *gnocchi* on a waxed-paper-lined baking sheet and place them in the freezer until hard. Once hard, transfer them to a plastic bag, and return them to the freezer until needed. Alternatively, you can prepare the entire dish ahead of time. Place the cooked *gnocchi* in an ovenproof casserole, cover it tightly, and freeze until needed. After thawing at room temperature for 1 hour, the dish bakes in 15 minutes at 375 degrees; if placed directly in the oven from the freezer, the cooking time is 30 minutes.

WHAT TO DRINK

Any dry, relatively light wine suits this meal. The cook prefers a Valpolicella or Bardolino. For a white wine, either a Soave or Frascati is a good choice.

SHOPPING LIST AND STAPLES

10-ounce package frozen chopped spinach
¾ pound fresh green beans
½ pound red potatoes
1 pint cherry tomatoes
Medium-size red onion
Small yellow onion
Medium-size clove garlic
Small bunch parsley
Large egg
1 stick unsalted butter
½ pound Parmesan cheese
8-ounce container whole-milk ricotta cheese
16-ounce can cannellini beans
½ cup good-quality olive oil, preferably virgin

3 tablespoons white wine vinegar, preferably French
1 tablespoon Dijon mustard
1 cup all-purpose flour, approximately
¼ teaspoon sugar
Freshly grated nutmeg
Salt
Freshly ground pepper

UTENSILS

Food processor (optional)
Stockpot
Large nonaluminum skillet
2 large saucepans
2 small saucepans
Large baking sheet
3 large bowls
Small bowl
Colander
Large strainer
Measuring cups and spoons
Chef's knife
Paring knife
Wooden spoons
Slotted spoon
Rubber spatula
Grater (if not using food processor)
Whisk
Garlic press (optional)

START-TO-FINISH STEPS

One hour ahead: Set out frozen spinach to thaw for gnocchi recipe.

1. Follow salad recipe steps 1 through 10.
2. Follow gnocchi recipe steps 1 through 13.
3. Follow salad recipe step 11 and serve with gnocchi.

RECIPES

Spinach Gnocchi with Butter and Parmesan

10-ounce package frozen chopped spinach, thawed
Small yellow onion
Medium-size clove garlic
1 stick unsalted butter
Large egg

¾ cup whole-milk ricotta cheese
Salt
Freshly ground pepper
½ pound Parmesan cheese
½ teaspoon freshly grated nutmeg
1 cup all-purpose flour, approximately

1. Bring 4 quarts water to a boil in stockpot over high heat.
2. Meanwhile, cook spinach in small saucepan according to package directions just until it separates; drain well and set aside.
3. Peel onion and finely chop enough to measure 1 tablespoon. Peel garlic and crush in garlic press or with chef's knife.
4. Melt 2 tablespoons butter in large nonaluminum skillet over low heat. Add onion and garlic and sauté 3 to 4 minutes, or until lightly colored. Add spinach and increase heat to medium. Cook about 5 minutes, or until spinach begins to stick to sides of skillet.
5. As spinach cooks, separate egg, placing yolk in large bowl and reserving white for another use. Add ricotta, ½ teaspoon salt, and ¼ teaspoon pepper to bowl with egg yolk and stir to combine.
6. Using food processor or grater, finely grate Parmesan cheese. Add 1 cup Parmesan to ricotta mixture; stir well.
7. Remove skillet with spinach from heat and stir in ¼ teaspoon nutmeg. Stir spinach into ricotta mixture.
8. Add ⅔ cup flour to ricotta mixture and stir well. Feel dough and add only enough additional flour so that dough holds together and does not stick to hands.
9. Line large baking sheet with waxed paper. Heavily flour work surface and hands. Using scant tablespoon dough for each, roll dough with hands into 50 to 60 small balls and place on waxed-paper-lined baking sheet.
10. When water boils, add 1 teaspoon salt. Add gnocchi, one at a time, and allow water to return to a gentle boil. Boil gently another 2 minutes. With slotted spoon, remove cooked gnocchi to colander.
11. Drain gnocchi well. Place drained gnocchi in large bowl, add 3 tablespoons butter, and stir gently.
12. In small saucepan over medium heat, brown remaining 3 tablespoons butter, and ¼ teaspoon each salt, pepper, and freshly grated nutmeg.
13. Sprinkle gnocchi with seasoned butter and ½ cup Parmesan. Divide gnocchi among 4 dinner plates and serve remaining Parmesan separately.

Mixed Vegetable Salad

Medium-size red onion
Small bunch parsley
16 cherry tomatoes
¾ pound fresh green beans
¼ teaspoon sugar
Salt
½ pound red potatoes
16-ounce can cannellini beans
½ cup good-quality olive oil, preferably virgin
3 tablespoons white wine vinegar, preferably French
1 tablespoon Dijon mustard
½ teaspoon freshly ground pepper

1. Bring 2 quarts water to a boil over high heat in each of 2 large saucepans.
2. Meanwhile, peel onion. Cut 3 to 4 thin slices crosswise from center of onion and separate into rings; set aside. Reserve remaining onion for another use. Wash parsley and dry with paper towels. Finely chop enough parsley to measure 2 tablespoons; set aside.
3. Wash and dry cherry tomatoes. Remove stems, if necessary. Set tomatoes aside.
4. Wash green beans and trim ends. Halve beans crosswise.
5. Add sugar and ¼ teaspoon salt to one pan of boiling water. Add green beans and boil about 5 minutes, or until crisp-tender. Turn beans into colander and refresh under cold running water; drain well.
6. Meanwhile, scrub potatoes and cut into ¼-inch-thick slices. Add potatoes to other pan of boiling water and boil about 5 minutes, or until just tender when pierced with tip of sharp knife.
7. While potatoes are cooking, turn cannellini beans into large strainer. Rinse beans briefly under cold running water and drain well. Combine cannellini beans and drained green beans in large bowl.
8. When cooked, drain potatoes and add to bowl with beans.
9. Add red onion rings, parsley, and cherry tomatoes to other vegetables.
10. Prepare dressing: In small bowl, whisk together olive oil, vinegar, mustard, pepper, and ½ teaspoon salt. Pour dressing over vegetables and toss. Set salad aside at room temperature until ready to serve.
11. To serve, toss salad again and divide among dinner plates.

Acknowledgments

The Editors would like to thank the following for their courtesy in lending items for photography: *Cover:* flatware—Buccellati; plate—Bennington Pottery. *Frontispiece:* white bowl, bread board—Wolfman-Gold & Good Co.; tiles—Country Floors; basket, boxes—Be Seated. *Pages 16–17:* pasta platter, appetizer tray—Japan Interiors Gallery; tray, glasses—Ad Hoc Housewares; flatware—Gorham. *Pages 20–21:* chili bowl, basket, napkin—Wolfman-Gold & Good Co.; glasses—Gorham. *Page 23:* tablecloth—Rosen; napkin, dishes—Broadway Panhandler. *Pages 26–27;* napkin, napkin ring, salsa bowl—Wolfman-Gold & Good Co. *Page 30:* platter, pitcher—Gear; spoon—Gorham. *Page 33:* plates, napkins—Gear. *Pages 36–37:* plates—Jenny B. Goode; salad plates, glasses, pitcher—Amigo Country; rug—Conran's. *Page 40:* tablecloth—Liberty of London; platters, mat—Gear; pan—Calphalon. *Page 42:* mug, plates—Claire Des Becker. *Pages 44–45:* tiles—Nemo Tile; flatware—Wallace Silversmiths; platter—Feu Follet. *Page 48:* fork—Gorham; bowl, plate—Baccarat. *Page 57:* fork—Gorham; plates—Columbus

Avenue General Store. *Page 58:* casseroles—Louis Lourioux; tiles—Nemo Tile. *Page 61:* plates—Dan Bleier; glasses—Gorham. *Pages 64–65:* soup bowl, ramekins—Pottery Barn; flatware—Gorham; napkin—Susskind Collection; tablecloth—China Seas; plate—Julien Mousa-Oghli. *Page 68:* spoon—Gorham; bowls—Conran's; napkin, tablecloth—China Seas. *Page 71:* platters—Pottery Barn; flatware—Gorham; napkin, tablecloth—China Seas. *Pages 74–75:* dishes, obi—Japan Interiors Gallery; flatware—Gorham. *Page 78:* dishes—Mikasa. *Page 81:* plates—Mikasa. *Pages 84–85:* dessert glasses, plate—Pan American Phoenix; tablecloth—Handloom Batik Importers. *Page 88:* plate—Gear; napkin—Pan American Phoenix. *Page 91:* plate—Pan American Phoenix. *Pages 94–95:* plate, mat—Ceramica Mia; fork—Wallace Silversmiths. *Page 98:* napkin—Wolfman-Gold & Good Co.; plate, table linen—Ceramica Mia; flatware—Wallace Silversmiths. *Page 100:* fork—Buccellati; napkin, marble underplate—Zona; plate, glass—Wolfman-Gold & Good Co.; tabletop—Formica® Brand Laminate by Formica Corp.

Kitchen equipment courtesy of: White-Westinghouse, Commercial Aluminum Cookware Co., Robot-Coupe, Caloric, Kitchen-Aide, J.A. Henckels Zwillingswerk, Inc., and Schwabel Corp. Microwave oven compliments of Litton Microwave Cooking Products.

Illustrations by Ray Skibinski
Production by Giga Communications
Photograph of Vicki Poth, page 4, by Ken Shung

Mail-Order Sources for Rice

Japanese Sweet Rice:
Wehah Farm, Inc.
P.O. Box 369
Richvale, CA 95974
(916) 882-4551

Basmati Rice:
House of Rice
4112 University Way N.E.
Seattle, WA 98105
(206) 633-5181

Index

Egg(s), 10
    crêpes with mushrooms and
        bean sprouts, 74, 78–80
    hard-boiled, with sesame green
        beans, 64, 71–73
    shirred, with mushrooms and
        artichokes, 64, 68–70
eggplant
    broiled, with *miso* sauce, 74,
        81–83
    canapés, 16–19
    salad with basil and lemon,
        44–47
    spiced, with mango chutney,
        85, 91–93
enchiladas, cheese, 37–39

Fat
    cooking safely with, 8
    sautéing with, 10
fennel, 35 *illus.*
    and watercress soup, 44, 48–49
feta-yogurt sauce with *bryami*,
    26, 33–35
figs, dried, with chèvre and
    almonds, 44–47
Forem, Ursula, 5
    menus of, 74–83
French-style dishes
    pan bagna with green sauce,
        44–47
fresh produce, 8
fritters, corn, with red pepper
    purée, 26, 30–32
fruit
    and coconut slices, 35
    and ice cream *tempura*, 80
    salad with jalapeño-lime
        dressing,
        64, 71–73
    see also names of fruits

Garlic sauce with braised
    tomatoes
        and chilies, 85, 88–90
gazpacho, 55–57
ginger in curried lentil soup,
    44, 51–53
gnocchi, spinach, with butter and
    Parmesan, 94, 100–102
goat cheese, *see* chèvre
grains, 9
grapefruit and honey dressing
    with vegetable and
        mushroom salad, 16–19
Greek-style dishes
    bryami with feta-yogurt sauce,
        26, 33–35
    green beans, sesame, with hard-
        boiled eggs, 64, 71–73
    green sauce with *pan bagna*,
        44–47
    guacamole salad, 55–57

Hash, vegetable, with salsa Rio
    Piña, 37, 40–41
herbed vegetables, 55, 58–60
honey and grapefruit dressing
    with vegetable and
        mushroom salad, 16–19

hot chocolate, Mexican, 42–43

Ice, tangerine, 53
ice cream and fruit *tempura*, 80
Indian-style dishes
    basmati rice, 85–87
    braised tomatoes with chilies
        in garlic sauce,
        85, 88–90
    carrot and mango relish, 87
    cream pudding, 85–87
    curried lentil soup with ginger,
        44, 51–53
    fresh Indian cheese with bell
        peppers, 85, 91–93
    Madras vegetable stew, 85–87
    pilaf, 85, 91–93
    pilaf, fragrant vegetable, 85,
        88–90
    raita, 44, 51–53
    raita, zucchini, 85, 88–90
    spiced eggplant with mango
        chutney, 85, 91–93
Italian-style dishes
    arugula and radicchio salad
        with warm mushroom
        dressing, 55, 61–63
    braised tomatoes, 55, 61–63
    manicotti with five cheeses, 94,
        98–99
    mixed vegetable salad, 94,
        100–102
    pasta Florentine, 55, 61–63
    pesto lasagna, 94–97
    spinach *gnocchi* with butter
        and Parmesan,
        94, 100–102
    tossed salad with Parmesan
        vinaigrette, 94, 98–99

Jalapeño-lime dressing with fruit
    salad, 64, 71–73
jambalaya, vegetable, 64, 71–73
Japanese-style dishes
    broiled eggplant with *miso*
        sauce, 74, 81–82
    cucumber salad with rice
        vinegar dressing, 77
    curried vegetable stew, 74–77
    egg crêpes with mushrooms
        and bean sprouts,
        74, 87–80
    fruit and ice cream *tempura*,
        80
    pan-fried tofu with vegetables,
        74, 81–83
    soba noodles with peanut sauce
        and spinach, 74, 78–80
    steamed rice, 76–77
    sweet and sour rice, 74, 81–83
    sweet potato-chestnut balls, 83
    vegetable salad with tofu-
        tahini dressing, 74, 78–79
    watercress rolls, 76–77
Johnson, Linda M., 4
    menus of, 16–19
Jones, Jeanne, 5
    menus of, 55–63

Lasagna, pesto, 94–97
legumes, 8
lentil soup, curried, with ginger,
    44, 51–53
lime-jalapeño dressing with fruit
    salad, 64, 71–73

Madison, Deborah, 4
    menus of, 44–53
Madras vegetable stew, 85–87
mango and carrot relish, 87
chutney with spiced eggplant,
    85, 91–93
manicotti with five cheeses, 94,
    98–99
Massie, John Robert, 5
    menus of, 64–73
Mexican-style dishes
    cheese *enchiladas*, 37–39
    cumin rice, 37–39
    gazpacho, 55–57
    guacamole salad, 55–57
    hot chocolate, 42–43
    spicy bean dip, 37, 40–41
    tamale pie, 55–57
    tomatillo salad, 37–39
    tropical salad, 37, 42–43
    vegetable hash with salsa Rio
        Piña, 37, 40–41
    vermicelli with walnut sauce,
        37, 42–43
miso sauce with broiled eggplant,
    74, 81–83
mozzarella and fresh coriander in
    tomato soup, 64, 68–70
mushroom(s)
    and bean sprouts with egg
        crêpes, 74, 78–80
    dressing, warm, with arugula
        and radicchio salad,
        55, 61–63
    and vegetable salad with
        honey-grapefruit
        dressing, 16–19
    wild, with shirred eggs and
        artichokes, 64, 68–70

Noodles, 8
    soba, with peanut sauce and
        spinach, 74, 78–80
nutburgers with fresh coriander
    salsa, 26–29
nuts, 10
    see also names of nuts

Pan bagna with green sauce,
    44–47
pancakes, vegetable, with yogurt
    sauce, 16, 23–25
pan frying, 10
pantry, 12–13
Parmesan
    and butter with spinach
        gnocchi, 94, 100–102
    popovers, 16, 20–22
    vinaigrette with tossed salad,
        94, 98–99
parsley salad with tarragon vin-
    aigrette, 55, 58–59

pasta, 8–10
    Florentine, 55, 61–63
    manicotti with five cheeses, 94,
        98–99
    pesto lasagna, 94–97
    with stir-fried vegetables,
        16–19
    vermicelli with walnut sauce,
        37, 42–43
    see also noodles
peanut
    sauce and spinach with *soba*
        noodles, 74, 78–80
    soup, creamy, 64–67
pears, baked, with almond filling,
    50
pesto lasagna, 94–97
pilaf, 85, 91–93
    vegetable, fragrant, 85, 88–90
pizza crêpes with tomatoes,
    zucchini,
        and goat cheese, 64–67
popovers, Parmesan, 16, 20–22
potatoes, *see* sweet potatoes
Poth, Vicki, 4
    menus of, 26–29
pot pie, vegetable, 26, 30–32
Pucci, Robert, 5
    menus of, 94–102
pudding, cream, Indian, 85–87

Radish and spinach salad, 16,
    20–22
raita, 44, 51–53
    zucchini, 85, 88–90
radicchio, 63 *illus.*
    and arugula salad with warm
        mushroom dressing,
        55, 61–63
red pepper
    purée with corn fritters, 26,
        30–32
    soup, creamy, 16, 23–25
relish, carrot and mango, 87
rice
    basmati, 85–87
    cumin, 37–39
    mail-order sources for, 103
    steamed, 76–77
    sweet and sour, 74, 81–83
    see also pilaf
rice vinegar dressing with
    cucumber salad, 77

Safety notes, 8
Sahni, Julie, 5
    menus of, 85–93
salad
    artichoke, 44, 48–50
    arugula and radicchio with warm
        mushroom dressing, 55, 61–63
    cucumber, with rice vinegar
        dressing, 77
    eggplant, with basil and lemon,
        44–47
    fruit, with jalapeño-lime dressing,
        64, 71–73
    grated carrot, 94–97
    guacamole, 55–57

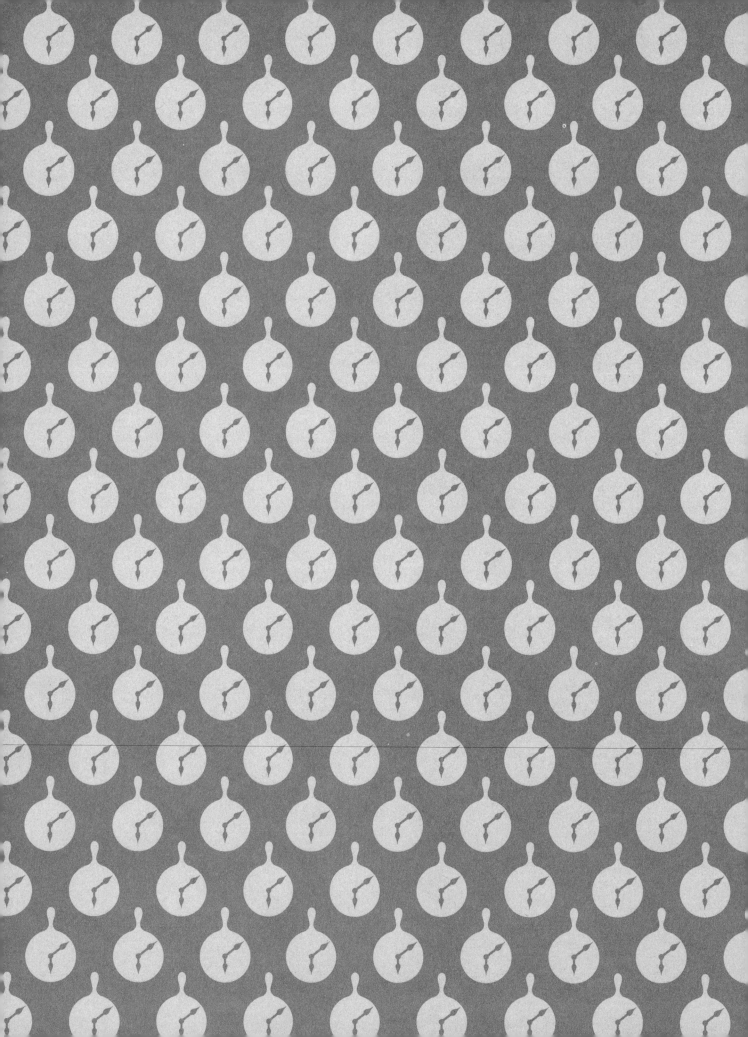